Betrayed Armenia

Diana Agabeg Apcar

Betrayed Armenia

Copyright © 2022 Indo-European Publishing

All rights reserved

The present edition is a reproduction of previous publication of this classic work. Minor typographical errors may have been corrected without note; however, for an authentic reading experience the spelling, punctuation, and capitalization have been retained from the original text.

ISBN: 978-1-64439-691-9

When this book was written, the writer was under the supposition then generally current that the Armenian Massacres of April, 1909, in Cilicia were instigated by Abdul Hamid and his Yildiz Clique. Babikian Effendi, the Armenian deputy who went to Adana from Constantinople to investigate into the massacres, plainly reported that all investigations had failed to trace them to Abdul Hamid and his Yildiz Clique. Babikian Effendi, as was to be expected, died suddenly on his return to Constantinople, but later on it became known that the massacres of April, 1909, had been planned, prepared, organized and carried into execution by the Constitutional Government of what has been called "Liberal Turks" or "Young Turks."

THEY TORE THE BABES FROM THE ARMS OF THEIR MOTHERS, TO HACK THEM TO PIECES WITH KNIVES, OR THROW THEM ALIVE INTO THE FIRE

CONTENTS

Why and Wherefore 2
Disinterested Evidence 5
Preface to 2nd Printing 10
Introduction 11

Part I

The Armenian Massacres and the Treaty of Berlin 25
The Armenian Massacres and the Turkish Constitution 35
The Armenian Massacres and the Armenian People 49
The Armenian Massacres and the Future of the 55
Armenians 62
The Armenian Massacres and Civilized Europe 73

Part II

Out of the Depths 73
What the Turkish Constitution Means for the Armenians 76
The Armenian Question 79
Open Letter to the Honorable President William Howard Taft 83
Abdul Hamid, the Triumph of Crime 87
L'Avenir 90
The Origin of the Armenians—The Introduction of Christianity into Armenia—Decline and Grand Revival . 94

WHY AND WHEREFORE

In making a study of my race, I have found three marked characteristics Intelligence—Energy—Industry. Combined with these three characteristics is an intense Love of Nationality. We live in a complex world. In an independent people these characteristics and this sentiment are laudable Virtues. In a subject people they are Crimes.

After I had laid this bitter Truth to heart, I did not have to seek for the Why and Wherefore of the Armenian Massacres.

The Armenian Massacres stand without their parallel in history. The human mind staggers to contemplate the fiendish orgies of which they have been the victims, and no pen can describe their horrors: and this helpless christian people are to-day in the same deadly peril as they have been since the famous Treaty of Berlin consigned them bound hand and foot to the mercy of their executioners.

The Armenians may be led again "as sheep to the slaughter" and the work of extermination may be completed—Jesus Christ was crucified on Calvary and the servant is not greater than his Lord—but the work of their extermination can only be completed when the evil influences in the Turkish Empire have reached their culminating point. Hitherto the Powers of Europe have by their jealousies and rivalries cultivated these evil influences, they have watered them and made them grow, but when their culminating point is reached, they must re-act on Christendom and the natural consequence must follow. Those who sow the wind, must reap the whirlwind. It is in the natural order of things.

I will allow that Liberty, Justice, Equality, Fraternity are the watchwords of Young Turkey, but Young Turkey is only a small minority; the great majority of the Turkish nation are not Young Turks.

The question therefore resolves itself into this critical point: "What will Christendom do even now?"

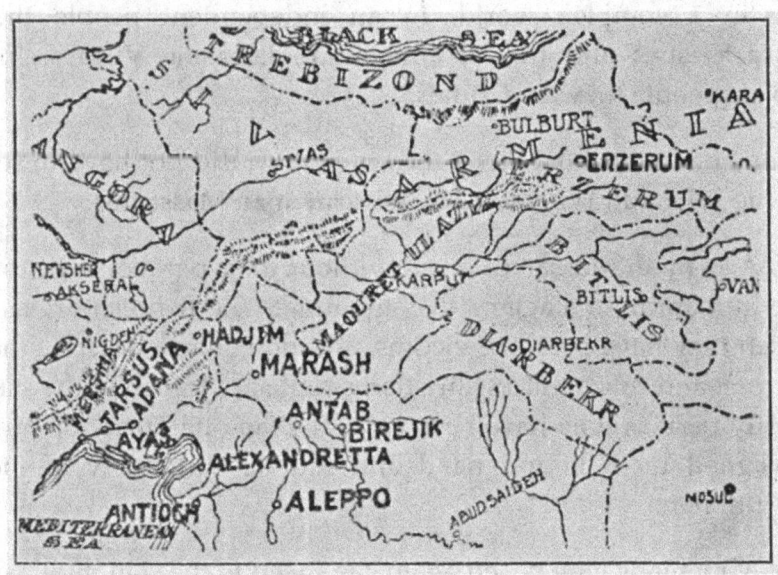

SCENE OF THE MASSACRES IN ASIA MINOR

The trouble began in Adana. An armed mob strengthened and augmented by soldiers fell in overwhelming numbers upon the unarmed Christians. The Armenian population of Antioch and vicinity were practically wiped out and the Armenian villages in the Alexandretta district destroyed with immense loss of life. Hadjim, Kessab and the neighbouring villages were burned. The Armenian quarter in Tarsus was ruined and ill-omened Marash stained again with the blood of thousands of Armenians. Zeitoon was desolated. The entire population of Kirikon between Aleppo and Alexandretta were massacred to the last babe. The mob and the soldiers burned what they could not carry away, so that the material loss has been enormous. In place of the former abundance and thriving industries there are instead desolated provinces and the charred and blackened remains of pillaged and ruined homes, and the residue of those who escaped massacre are reduced to homelessness and starvation.

DISINTERESTED EVIDENCE

I have thought it advisable to insert a few extracts from accounts of the Massacres of April, 1909, given by disinterested witnesses.

IN THIS HOUSE 115 WOMEN AND CHILDREN WERE ROASTED ALIVE

> *History repeats itself. In 1895 Turkish soldiers fell upon seventy to eighty young women and girls in a church, where they had fled for refuge, and after hideously outraging them, barricaded them in, setting fire to the building at the same time, and derisively shouting to their victims as they were being roasted alive, to call upon their Christ to save them now.*

"We are having a perfectly hideous time here. Thousands have been murdered—25,000 in this province they say; but the number is probably greater, for every Christian village was wiped out. In Adana about 5000 have perished. After Turks and Armenians had made peace, the Turks came in the night with hose and kerosene, and set fire to what remained of the Armenian quarter. Next day the French and Armenian schools were fired. Nearly everyone in the Armenian school perished, anybody trying to escape being shot down by the soldiers."

"The Turkish Authorities do nothing except arrest unoffending Armenians, from whom by torture they extort the most fanciful confessions. Even the wounded are not safe from their injustice. A man was being carried in to me yesterday when he was seized and taken off to gaol. I dare not think what his fate may be."

"For fiends incarnate commend me to the Turks. Nobody is safe from them. They murder babies in front of their mothers; they half murder men, and violate the wives while the husbands are lying there dying in pools of blood."

"The authorities did nothing, and the soldiers were worse than the crowd, for they were better armed. One house in our quarter was burned with 115 people inside. We counted the bodies. The soldiers set fire to the door, and as the windows had iron bars, nobody could get out. Everybody in the house was roasted alive. They were all women and children and old people."—Extract from letter of Mrs. Doughty-Wylie, wife of British Consul at Adana; published in the London "Daily Mail."

"The soldiers led the way in these horrors and were guilty of atrocities so terrible that they can never be described in a public print. Even the soldiers landed at Mersina—the soldiers sent expressly to restore order—added to the crimes and for three days continued the murders unchecked."—Extract from the London "Daily Mail."

RUINED CHURCH AND HOMES AT ADANA

"The outbreak began in the Armenian bazaar on April 14th, and on the pretence that an Armenian revolt was in progress the Redifs or reserves were called out. These, as villainous a crew as could well be found, had arms and ammunition served out to them, and immediately joined in the slaughter, and all the worst of the subsequent killing, looting, and house burning was done by them."

"The Armenians did not take their punishment lying down. Their quarter of the town was so well defended that the mob, mad as they were with lust for blood, would not venture into it. Houses on the outskirts were besieged by thousands of men and held by half a dozen; in fact, the courage of these hordes of Moslem savages was only equal to butchering women and children and unarmed men. I saw a Greek house which was held for eight hours by one Armenian with a shotgun against hundreds of Turks firing from the surrounding houses and the minaret of a mosque. At last his cartridges gave-out, but not for two hours after that did the mob pluck up courage to rush the house."—Extracts from accounts by Mr. J. L. C. Booth, special correspondent of the London "Graphic."

"Kessab was a thrifty Armenian town of about eight thousand inhabitants, situated on the landward slope of Mt. Cassius (Arabic, Jebel Akra) which stands out prominently upon the Mediterranean seacoast half-way between Alexandretta and Latakia. Kessab is now a mass of blackened ruins, the stark walls of the churches and houses rising up out of the ashes and charred timbers heaped on every side. What must it mean to the five thousand men and women and little children who have survived a painful flight to the seacoast and have now returned to their mountain home, only to find their houses sacked and burned! There were nine Christian villages which clustered about Kessab in the valleys below. Several of these have been completely destroyed by fire. All have been plundered and the helpless people driven out or slain."

"Can you imagine the feelings of the Kessab people as they climbed on foot the long trail up the mountain, and then as they came over the ridge into full view of their charred and ruined dwellings? Their stores of wheat, barley and rice had been burned; clothing, cooking utensils, furniture and tools had gone; their goats, cows and mules had been stolen; their silk industries stamped out; their beloved churches reduced to smouldering heaps. The bodies of their friends and relatives who had been killed had not been buried. And yet the love of home is so strong that the people have settled down there with the determination to clear up the debris and rebuild their houses."—Extracts from "The Sack of Kessab," Stephen Van R. Trowbridge.

As these sheets are going through the press there comes news of famine at Zeitoon. The Rev. F. W. Macullum, American Missionary at Marash, writes to the Rev. W. W. Peet, American Missionary at Constantinople, that 12,000 souls in and around Zeitoon are dying of hunger; they are wandering about in rags, mixing bran and water, and cooking and eating it, if they can get even that. Rev. Macullum adds, "The same story comes to us from all sides. As we foresaw all along, from now on the distress will be greatest."

If 50,000 were massacred, the list of those who have died and are dying of homelessness and starvation will exceed 150,000. It is true; and the numbers are not exaggerated. Last year the people reaped no harvest, and this year there are no sowings.

The latest news is that Mush, a prosperous Armenian village that had escaped the desolation of the massacres, has been plundered in a night attack by armed Kurds, and the villagers are now reduced to extreme distress. Before the outbreak the Armenian patriarchal vicar at Mush had repeatedly appealed to the Armenian Patriarch at Constantinople, and the Armenian Patriarch had repeatedly appealed to the Authorities at Constantinople asking protection for the villagers of Mush as a Kurdish attack was apprehended. It is evident that the authorities at Constantinople are unable to protect thriving Armenian villages from Kurdish and Turkish raiders.

PREFACE TO 2ND PRINTING

The first and second parts of this little book were written and printed in pamphlet form for circulation in the United States, shortly after the Adana Massacres of April, 1909. I have now thought it advisable to add a Supplement of a short history of the Origin of the Armenians and the Introduction and Revival of Christianity in Armenia.

The illustrations and the extracts from the periodicals "Harper's Monthly," "The Wide World" and the "Cosmopolitan" have been added to the 2nd printing.

INTRODUCTION TO 2ND PRINTING

My object in writing this little book is to lay the hard case of my unfortunate race before the men and women of the United States; since it is from the United States that the American Missionaries have gone forth, who have been the only helping influence from without for my suffering people in Asiatic Turkey. To the earnest and devoted men and women of the American Missions, we Armenians owe a debt of gratitude which we can never repay.

If in the contents of the pages of this little book I have exaggerated Facts by one whit or one iota, if I have deviated by one hair's breadth from the Truth, I stand to be judged.

"God save us from another Adana, but the sword of Islam has not been dulled" was one of the clarion notes sounded at the Sixth International Convention of the Student Volunteer Movement, which was held at Rochester, New York. The man who sounded that clarion note knew Islam, and because knowing of my own knowledge that the sword of Islam has not been dulled, I tremble lest its sharp edge fall once more on the neck of my helpless race. If I knew and felt sure in mine own heart that the sword of Islam was dulled, I would be content to let bygones be bygones, and to hold my peace and be silent for ever.

Like the sudden explosion of a volcano in the physical world, comes the explosion of a Turkish Massacre of Armenians in the moral world. It comes just in that way; the subterranean fires are always there, but all of a sudden the sulphur flames of religious fanaticism burst, the lava floods of race hatred and lust of plunder, break forth and run in fiery streams; the unfortunate victims are pounced upon, swooped upon, pillaged, plundered, butchered, slaughtered, subjected to outrages so hideous, cruel, loathsome, and revolting, that no pen could depict their horrible realities and the details can never go into print. The human mind is staggered and asks itself the question if even the imaginations of fiends and devils could originate such horrors. Then this orgy of the human fiends is arrested. For the time being the appetite for blood, lust, and plunder is satisfied; for the time being, the eye is content with the scenes of havoc and desolation lying under the sun; the smell of corpses is in the air, the odor from the carcases of the "christian swine" reek in the nostrils of the Turk, he turns away, his jaws dripping with blood, and rests to couch for a future spring. We have seen that sort of an end to the tragedy of a tiger's victim: the tiger has eaten his fill, he rests, to keep guard over the crunched bones and mangled bits of bloody flesh that bestrew the earth. So also now there is a residue left of those that have served as the meat and wine of this devil's feast; the demons have gorged themselves over the banquet, and now there are left over the broken remains of the banquet, the miserable residue homeless and destitute.

Civilized nations have received a temporary moral shock, like a shock that spreads from the centre of an explosion; the electric vibration running far and wide from the scene of the centre of devastation. There are among these civilized nations generous and kind-hearted people who open their purse strings; they give money to purchase shelter, food and clothing for these homeless, naked and hungry beggars, made homeless, naked and hungry through no fault of their own. But oh! ye generous and kind hearted people! can any power under heaven assuage the heart anguish of this miserable residue? Can they be made by any means of human comfort to forget the black horrors or recover from the effects of the fires of the hideous affliction through which they have passed? What is there left for a woman who has seen with her own eyes the slaughter and heard with her own ears the dying cry of her murdered child? even her reason must give way under the stress of her anguish. All ye who are mothers, I appeal to you, for one moment to put yourselves in the place of thousands of such mothers, in whose hearts the same mother's love burns as in yours, and then measure the depth of their agony.

Generous and kind hearted people who open your purse strings; would to God I entreat, ye would raise up your voices and demand that this hideous slaughter and oppression of a helpless christian race should cease. Would to God I entreat, ye would raise up your voices and demand that this people of an industrious, intelligent christian race, robust in mind and body, should be let to live. Would to God I entreat, that ye would raise up your voices and demand for them that security of life and property to which they are entitled just as equally as all other peoples.

Public Sentiment has done great things in the world's history. Public Sentiment liberated Greece, The Lebanon, The Balkan States from Turkish Oppression. Slavery was abolished in the United States through Public Sentiment: but alas! does Public Sentiment sleep for this helpless Christian race. Are they not God's creatures? have they not a right to live on God's earth as other nations? Does Humanity, does Christianity allow that tender babes and children should be hideously and horribly mutilated and butchered before the eyes of their mothers, or that the ears of mothers should be rent with the cries of the dying agony of their murdered children? Does Humanity, does Christianity allow that helpless women should be forcibly subjected to the most hideous, the most loathsome, the most revolting, and the most cruel outrages? Does Humanity, does Christianity, allow all this?

Christian Governments have organized a Hague Conference of Peace and Civilization, but they have closed its doors to the cause of a bleeding christian race groaning under the yoke of the cruellest oppressors that the world has yet known. Christian men and women have held up their hands in horror at the Indian Juggernauth; but alas! the political wheels of Christian Governments have been a Greater Juggernauth for a helpless christian race. It is by Christian Governments that "we are made as the filth of the world, and as the offscouring of all things unto this day." It is as if the answer to our groanings had been made by Christian Governments in just these words:

"We know that you have had frightful grievances, such as have been beyond the measure of human endurance. We know that since the Treaty of Berlin your history has been written in blood and tears, as the history of no other nation has been written before or now. We know that your women are subjected to the most revolting and hideous agonies, and your babes and children hounded to hideous deaths. We know that the sum total of your wrongs and sufferings is so great, that the cry of its anguish is piercing the very heavens, but really, our political and commercial jealousies prevent; and we each one of us being on the look out lest our separate political and commercial interests in the Empire of your oppressors be endangered, cannot regard you. It may be the deadliest scandal of Christendom that we Christian Powers should be all gathered together, one against another, in the Empire of your Oppressors, as eagles gather together round a carcase; but really there is no help for it; and if you must die hideously by a hellish extermination, why then you must die, and we have to condone your hellish extermination, for in any case, each one of us must secure his own political and commercial interests in this same Empire of your Oppressors."

In "Transcaucasia and Ararat," published by Mr. James Bryce in 1876, there occurs in the chapter entitled "Some Political Reflections" the following passage:

"The attention of the West was so much drawn towards Herzegovina and Bulgaria by the events of 1876 that the miseries of the Asiatic subjects of the Porte have been unreasonably forgotten or neglected. They are fully as wretched as the Slavs or Cretans have been; and in so far worse off, that in Europe there exists no large body of tribes making murder and robbery its regular and daily occupation as the Kurds, and latterly the Circassians also, have done in Armenia. If anyone will take the trouble to read the complaints of oppressions and cruelties presented to the Porte by the Armenian Patriarchate in 1872 (since reprinted in England) and some of the more recent statements printed by the Armenians in England on the same topic, he will see that the state of Turkish Asia presents as grave and pressing a problem as that of Bulgaria itself."

In the 4th edition of the same book, published in 1896, the following note appears to the passage I have quoted:

"Shortly after this was written, the Blue Books presented to Parliament, containing reports from British Consuls in Asiatic Turkey, showed that things were really far worse there than they had been in Bulgaria or Herzegovina."

What has followed since 1876 is too well known. For seeking redress from their frightful grievances the Armenians were hunted like wild beasts and killed like rats and flies during the Hamidian régime.

You will tell me, my christian friends, that with the rise of the reform party in Turkey, the era of massacres is at an end, and I will tell you that the conditions of 1876 and 1896 have not actually changed, though they may seemingly appear so to the uninformed and uninitiated. I will answer you that the hideous massacres of April last happened nine months after the reform party first rose in power, and nine months after the inauguration of the Constitution. I do not question the goodwill of the reform party, but the reform party does not comprise the whole Turkish nation, and until the Turk learns to become liberal, civilized and human, there may be no more Armenians left, unless some Christian Power such as the United States demands their protection and enforces it. No! my Christian friends, it can be well for other Christians in the Turkish Empire with their powerful Governments at their back; but alas! there is no security for a subject people alien in race and religion.

The massacres in April last raged from Adana to Alexandretta, and according to authenticated reports about fifty thousand men, women and children were hideously exterminated; more than this, the last massacres were especially characterized by the most hideous, the most loathsome, the most revolting and ferocious cruelties perpetrated on women and children. Now what other name can we find for the perpetrators of this diabolical orgy, except to call them fiends incarnate; and who is the bold man who can guarantee that these same fiends incarnate have become metamorphosed and changed all of a sudden; or that the handful of liberal Turks at Constantinople are capable of controlling and restraining them. We have not even heard that the leaders and participators of the last massacres have been punished as they deserved; and what is the reason they are left unpunished? because the Government is afraid to punish Mahommedans for killing Christians; because the liberal Turks dare not punish the "true believers" for killing "Kaffirs."

The religion of Mahommed, the religion of the sword, has been infused into the Turk, and to understand the effect of the religion of Mahommed upon the Turk, it is necessary to regard it from four aspects, or from four points of analysis. First, the fundamental doctrine and law of the religion. Second, the character of the founder as an example to his followers. Third, the racial and ethnographic characteristics of the Turk. Fourth, the effect which this particular religion would be likely to have on this particular race. When we have viewed the Turk and his government from these four points of analysis, we have the explanation of all the woe and desolation which have lain over the countries under Turkish rule.

"When ye encounter the unbelievers strike off their heads until you have made a great slaughter of them" is a chapter of the Koran which the Turk has religiously and steadfastly made his creed.

In conclusion, I will ask my readers to compare one point of difference between the two races, the oppressor and the oppressed. Thousands upon thousands of Armenian women, thousands upon thousands of Armenian children, have been hounded to death, or savagely, ferociously, horribly and loathsomely maltreated by the Turk, and yet in all the agonizing years when Massacre has succeeded upon Massacre, has there been one known case or one single instance of a Turkish woman or child maltreated by Armenians?

The last massacres though especially organized from the Palace at Constantinople, were officially announced to originate from an affray between one Armenian and three Turks, in which the single handed one, on the one side, grappling with the three on the other, killed one of the three: given equal numbers and arms, the Armenian is always a match for the Turk, but alas for him that unequal numbers and want of arms have always made him the victim of his oppressor.

Ahmed Riza Bey in the first part (Ses Causes) of his book "La Crise de L'Orient" published in Paris in 1907 holds a brief for his nation which through its own fallacious arguments falls to the ground. I will quote one passage as an example.

"Jamais les populations chrétiennes ne se sont révoltées, spontanément, d'elles-mêmes. Les révoltes ont toujours été partielles et espacées, ce qui tend bien à prouver qu'elles sont provoquées non par certains injustices administratives que nous savons être constantes et les mêmes pour tous, mais par les sourdes menées de l'extérieur. Les agences consulaires, les écoles étrangères, les maisons des missionnaires, couvertes par les Capitulations, ont servi de foyer de propagande, de dépôts d'armes, et même de refuge pour les perturbateurs. Souvent les ambassadeurs sont intervenus pour faire gracier des rebelles pris et condamnés. On se rappelle avec quelle solennité les Arméniens qui s'étaient introduits dans la Banque Ottomane furent conduits sains et saufs à bord d'un bateau par le drogman de l'Ambassade russe—leur complice.

"Si ces prétendus patriotards sont tant soutenus et choyés dans le monde occidental, c'est parce qu'ils constituent un élément ou plutôt un instrument de destruction au service de certains Européens élevés dans les préjugés des Croissades et qui crient avec Chateaubriand: ('L'espèce humaine ne peut que gagner à la destruction de l'Empire Ottoman')."

The author of "La Crise de L'Orient" continues in this strain. Are we then to suppose that the British Consuls, men whose truthfulness has never been impeached, whose reports on the unsupportable sufferings of the subject christian races and the oppressions and hideous atrocities of the Turks, have filled volumes: and likewise the American Missionaries, men who have deservedly gained the honor and respect of the world, whose statements have corroborated the British Consular reports; have been according to Ahmed Riza Bey the mischief-makers in the Turkish Empire? since it is from them alone the world has gained the widest and most correct knowledge of the daily miseries and oppressions under which the subject Christian races have groaned. Are we also to suppose that men like Mr. James Bryce and Dr. Dillon have by mendacious writings upheld them, British Consul and American Missionary, liars, and mischief makers? Or rather are we not to suppose that if thinking men and women in the world have come to cry out with Chateaubriand "L'espèce humaine ne peut que gagner à la destruction de l'Empire Ottoman" it is because the Turks have earned the world's condemnation through their own diabolical acts, and on account of the woe and desolation which Turkish rule has worked over the fairest provinces under the sun. If the Turk will turn from the evil of his ways unto good, the stigma of "the unspeakable Turk" which now attaches itself to him, will cease to be a veritable truth. The bringing about of the transformation rests with himself.

Further in answer to Ahmed Riza Bey's account of the Armenian "prétendus patriotards" in connection with the Ottoman Bank; I cannot do better than quote from Mr. Bryce's version of the story, and the massacre that followed: "In the following June serious trouble arose at Van, where some sort of insurrection is said to have been planned, though in the discrepancy of the accounts it is hard to arrive at the truth. Masses of Kurds came down threatening to massacre the Christians, and a conflict in which many innocent persons perished, was with difficulty brought to an end by the intervention of the British Consul. A little later the Armenian revolutionary party, emboldened by the rising in Crete, where the Christians, being well armed and outnumbering the Muslims, held their ground successfully, issued appeals to the Embassies and to the Turkish Government to introduce reforms, threatening disturbances if the policy of repression and massacre was persisted in. These threats were repeated in August, and ultimately, on August 26, a band of about twenty Armenians, belonging the revolutionary party, made a sudden attack on the Imperial Ottoman Bank in Constantinople, declaring they were prepared to hold it and blow it up should the Sultan refuse their demand. They captured the building by a *coup de main*, but were persuaded by the Russian dragoman to withdraw upon a promise of safety. Meanwhile the Government, who through their spies knew of the project, had organised and armed a large mob of Kurds and Lazes—many of whom had recently been brought to the city— together with the lowest Turkish class. Using the occasion, they launched this mob upon the peaceful Armenian population. The onslaught began in various parts of the city so soon after the attack on the Bank that it had obviously been prearranged, and the precaution had been taken to employ the Turkish ruffians in different quarters from those in which they dwelt; so that they might less easily be recognised. Carts had moreover been prepared in which to carry off the dead. For two days an indiscriminate slaughter went on, in which not only Armenian merchants and traders of the cultivated class, not only the industrious and peaceable Armenians of the humbler class, clerks, domestic servants, porters employed on the quays and in the warehouses, but also women and children were butchered in the streets and hunted down all through the suburbs. On the afternoon of the 27th the British Chargé d'Affaires (whose action throughout won general approval) told the Sultan he would land British sailors, and the Ambassadors telegraphed to the Sultan. Then the general massacre was stopped, though sporadic slaughter went on round the city during the next few days. The Ambassadors, who did not hesitate to declare that the massacre had been organised by the Government, estimated the number of killed at from 6000 to 7000; the official report made to the Sultan is said to have put it at 8750.[1] During the whole time the

---

[1] In a recent publication "Fifty Years in Constantinople," the author Dr. George Washburn, ex-President of Robert College, estimates the number that were slaughtered in cold blood in the streets of the city as 10,000. Dr. Washburn adds the following: "The massacre of the Armenians came to an end on Friday, the day after the soldiers came to the College; but the persecution of them which went on for months was worse than the massacre. Their business was destroyed, they were plundered and blackmailed without mercy, they were hunted like wild beasts, they were imprisoned, tortured, killed, deported, fled the

army and the police had perfect control of the city—the police, and a certain number of the military officers and some high civil officials, joining in the slaughter. Of all the frightful scenes which Constantinople, a city of carnage, has seen since the great insurrection of A.D. 527 when 30,000 people perished in the hippodrome there has been none more horrible than this. For this was not the suppression of an insurrection in which contending factions fought. It was not the natural sequel to a capture by storm, as when the city was taken and sacked by the Crusaders in A.D. 1204, and by the Turks in A.D. 1453. It was slaughter in cold blood, when innocent men and women, going about their usual avocations in a time of apparent peace, were suddenly beaten to death with clubs, or hacked to pieces with knives, by ruffians who fell upon them in the streets before they could fly to any place of refuge."[2]

I am also obliged to quote from an Article written by a Turkish Officer who signs himself A. J. and published in the "Siper-i-Saïka-i-Hurriet," a Turkish daily, on July 6, 1909.

> Every time that I hear the name Armenian I feel the bleeding of a moral wound within me. It was the year I was sent into exile (1896). On a Thursday, before we had left the Military School for our vacation, a rumor flew through the school,—"They are massacring the Armenians." All my young patriotic companions turned pale from deep emotion. Every one tried to read in the sad faces of others the reason for this bad news. But each one avoided expressing his thought. After a time the details began to circulate to the effect that the Armenians had dared to destroy the Ottoman Bank and

---

country, until the Armenian population of the city was reduced by some seventy-five thousand, mostly men, including those massacred."
[2] "Transcaucasia and Ararat: Twenty Years of the Armenian Question."—James Bryce.

government buildings with bombs, and that this was the reason why they were massacred. At that time all of us trembled, because we also were enemies of that government, because we also wished to overthrow it, and although we were not convinced that the best service could be rendered by bombs, we were working quietly to spread our ideas. In our hearts a flame of enmity and indignation, no less terrible than bombs, was burning. The poor Armenians were being massacred ruthlessly, because out of their number five or ten persons, resenting their wrongs, had rebelled. But that which maddened these poor men, that drove them to rebellion and placed bombs in their hands was the stupidity of the people and the outrageous oppressions of the government. And now this inhuman government was killing with clubs a noble nation, under the pretext of putting down a rebellion produced by its own oppressions. Among the crimes committed by the former government the most unpardonable crime was the Armenian massacre. If there was a race up to that time among non-Moslem peoples which with sincere and deep feeling honored the Ottoman fatherland that race was the Armenian. It is the Armenians who wear most nearly the national dress, who speak and write Turkish best, and recognize the Ottoman country as their fatherland. Besides this it is the Armenians who engage in commerce and agriculture, and thus, by demonstrating its fruitfulness, increase the value of the Ottoman Empire. Because a few among them justly started an agitation, these our noble and industrious brethren were being massacred. What a terrible scene! When we left the school building we saw hundreds of the bodies of our Armenian compatriots being removed in manure carts; legs and arms were hanging down outside. This bloody scene will ever remain impressed on my mind.

"This shocking crime of Yildiz formed a deep lake of blood, and this lake, during the whole course of a cursed absolutism, up to the last moment, grew wider. Even during the past nine months of the Constitution, in spite of the brotherly feelings which had been shown, the awful events in Adana took place and the souls of all true Osmanlis melted into tears. Up to the present time the deep sorrow caused by this event has not disappeared, because this bloody wound in our social body cannot easily be cured. While we fill our stomachs with choice morsels, while we rest selfishly in our comfortable beds, these fatherless and brotherless orphans, widows hungry, naked, and barefoot wander hither and thither, and thousands of families are fleeing from the fatherland. We are convinced that the government is doing its work, but what has happened is so great a calamity that it can keep a government busy for years. However much sacrifice we may make, still it will be inadequate, because the happiness of the fatherland depends on healing such blood wounds as these as soon as possible. We are convinced that the government and all connected with it are persuaded of this as well as ourselves. We must now wipe out the traces of the misfortune brought by a cursed period. We must now comfort weeping hearts. We must understand and teach those who do not understand that patriotism and brotherhood do not differ from each other. The responsibility of the government for the Armenians is very great and very weighty. The whole Ottoman nation is under obligations to protect this suffering race, because the liberty we enjoy to-day is in large part due to the blood shed by the Armenians. We thought that these truths were so obvious that we preferred to keep silence, whereas to-day we understand that it is necessary from time to time to recall the greatness of our obligation. We must not forget that this unhappy people up to yesterday has endured only barbarism, and for twelve years has been constantly oppressed and ground to the earth, and has given thousands of victims. Hereafter we must work to assure them that the era of massacres has passed, and with all our strength of mind and soul we must quiet them. The obligation of the government to protect them is also very heavy, because our Armenian countrymen live among wandering tribes. We must all assist the government and point out its obligation. It must be declared in public and periodically that the one of the most important duties of the Ottoman nation is to protect, together with those of other races, the interests, the life, and property of the Armenians as well, since these are their sacred rights. Let investigations be made and let whatever is necessary be done in order to reach this aim."

This article of the Turkish officer, who however does not dare disclose his identity; and the account given by an authority like Mr. James Bryce surely refute the facile explanation of Ahmed Riza Bey in alluding to the Massacres as "les Massacres occasionnés par les aventuriers Arméniens." Indeed it holds out poor hope for the furtherance of liberty and justice in Turkey when the man who is the President of the Chamber of Deputies only as far back as 1907 tries to palliate the horrors of the Hamidian régime by misrepresentations.

The author of "La Crise de l'Orient" also cites the Japanese as an instance of the civilization and aptitude for progress of a non-Christian oriental race. In this case, Ahmed Riza Bey certainly needs to measure the distance between the mental, moral and humane qualities of the Japanese and the Turk, a distance as great as lies geographically between the North Pole and the South.

PART I

THE ARMENIAN MASSACRES AND THE TREATY OF BERLIN

Since the gathering of the Plenipotentiaries of Europe at the famous Congress of Berlin in 1878, and the signing of the still more famous Treaty of Berlin, the martyr roll of the unfortunate Armenian nation stands without its parallel in history.

In the Guildhall at Berlin hangs a picture of the memorable scene witnessed in that city on July the thirteenth 1878. The painter has depicted the proud array of representatives of the powerful Governments of Europe, but in the interests of Humanity there should be attached to that painting the wording of Article 61 of the Treaty of Berlin written in letters of blood (Armenian blood).

It was a curious irony of Fate, that although the taking of "the terrible stronghold of Kars," universally admitted to be one of the greatest and most difficult military exploits ever achieved, and the crowning success of the Russian arms in Asiatic Turkey, should have been accomplished by an Armenian General; that although Armenian Generals in the Russian service had led to conquest, and Armenian soldiers fought, conquered and died, yet by these successes not only was no amelioration attained of the hard fate of their unhappy nation under Turkish rule, but that fate, hard before, was made a hundredfold and even a thousandfold harder.

GENERAL PRINCE LORIS MELIKOFF

Commanded the Russian forces in Asiatic Turkey during the Russo-Turkish war and captured the impregnable fortress of Kars. Appointed Prime Minister of Russia by Alexander II. The liberal policy which characterized the reign of that excellent monarch, and the Constitution that he was on the eve of granting to his people were influenced by Melikoff; but after the death of Alexander II he was not allowed to continue in his good work of reforming Russia, being overthrown from office early in the reign of Alexander III.

The efforts of the Armenians, and the entreaties of their Patriarch Nerses had procured the insertion of Article 16 in the Treaty of San Stefano signed between Russia and Turkey in March 1878. In fact the wording of the Article had been suggested by the Patriarch himself. It provided the following stipulation for the protection of the Armenians:—

"As the evacuation by the Russian troops of the territory which they now occupy in Armenia, and which is to be restored to

Turkey, might give rise to conflicts and complications detrimental to the maintenance of good relations between the two countries, the Sublime Porte engages to carry into effect without further delay the improvements and reforms demanded by local requirements in the provinces inhabited by the Armenians, and to guarantee their security against the Kurds and Circassians."

What followed has passed into history. The British Government of which Lord Beaconsfield (then Mr. D'Israeli) was Premier, and Lord Salisbury Foreign Secretary, once more pursued the old policy of baffling Russian aggrandizement in Turkey. Afraid that her own real or fancied interests would thereby become imperilled, England threw in the weight of her power, and virtually commanded the substitution of the Treaty of Berlin in lieu of the Treaty of San Stefano. Thus the substantial guarantee of a natural and immediate protector, both able and desirous of enforcing the protection which the Armenians then had in Russia, was taken away, and the security of impotent words given in its stead, namely:—

"The Sublime Porte undertakes to carry out without further delay the improvements and reforms demanded by local requirements in the provinces inhabited by the Armenians, and to guarantee their security against the Circassians and Kurds. It will periodically make known the steps taken to this effect to the Powers, who will superintend their application."

"It will periodically make known the steps taken to this effect to the Powers, who will superintend their application." How this last proviso could furnish food for laughter were it not for the terrible tragedy involved in it.

The insertion of Article 61 in the Treaty of Berlin, granted, or rather seemingly granted, by the six Powers of Europe, proved in reality, as subsequent events bore out, an instrument of death and torture. It was as if the reversal of the figures had reversed the possibilities of succour and protection, and with the death of the Czar Liberator, the last chance of the Armenians died.

The Turkish Massacres of 1875 and 1876 which led up to the Russo-Turkish War of 1877 are historical facts too well known to need further comment in this article. The Czar Liberator stands out in history as that noble figure—a benefactor of mankind. Through his humanitarian susceptibilities, and his sublime efforts for their deliverance, the Christians of European Turkey received immunity from Turkish slaughter; and the protection of his benevolent arm was extended over that unhappy Christian nation of Asiatic Turkey, the Armenians; at least it would have secured them immunity from the record-breaking slaughter that followed, but the Power that had stood behind Turkey since 1791 frustrated his endeavours.

A British commentator on that page of British policy has summed it up in the words:—

"In no other part of the world has our national policy or conduct been determined by motives so immoral and so stupid."[3]

The same commentator, in reviewing also the result of the substituted Treaty, fittingly remarks:—

"The Turk could see at a glance that, whilst it relieved him of the dangerous pressure of Russia, it substituted no other pressure which his own infinite dexterity in delays could not make abortive. As for the unfortunate Armenians, the change was simply one which must tend to expose them to the increased enmity of their tyrants, whilst it damaged and discouraged the only protection which was possible under the inexorable conditions of the physical geography of the country."

---

[3] "Our Responsibilities For Turkey."—Argyll (note to 2nd printing).

It had been the constant endeavour of the Patriarch Nerses to point out to the Armenians that their true policy lay in aiding Russian advance in Turkey: that even if Russia were selfish in her designs, she was the only Christian Power that would stand as their protector against Turkish or Persian tyranny. His political foresight had already been verified as early as 1827[4] and his strenuous life-long labours were nearing the goal in 1878, but were frustrated by the fatal action that intervened.

England, by commanding the substitution of the Treaty of Berlin in place of that of San Stefano had taken upon herself the heaviest obligations any nation could incur. It is unnecessary to repeat that those obligations were never fulfilled.

If the lamented death of the Emperor Alexander II was one of the most unhappy events that could have befallen Russia; it was a hundredfold more unhappy for the Armenian nation. His successor, who adopted repressive and coercive measures for his own people in the place of his father's liberal policy, not only applied the same measures to his Armenian subjects in his own domains, but left their countrymen under Turkish rule to their merciless fate.

Russia, twice foiled in her subjugation of Turkey, changed her policy from that of crushing into that of upholding the Ottoman Empire. When the horrors of the Armenian massacres, revealed to the people of England by their own ambassadors and consuls, their own journalists and men of letters, thrilled the hearts of

---

[4] In 1826 the Russian General Paskevitch defeated the Persians at Elizabetopol and in the following year 1827 he seized the monastery of Etchmiatzin (the seat of the Armenian Patriarch) and Erivan one of the great towns of Armenia and gained for himself the title of Erivanski. By these successes Russia advanced as far as the line of the Araxes and wrested from Persia the provinces of Erivan and Nakhitchvan. The Treaty of Peace was concluded between Russia and Persia at Turkmantchai on the 22nd of February 1828. — Note to 2nd printing.

men and women, when England's "Grand Old Man" thundered his vituperations against the "Great Assassin,"[5] Prince Lobanoff in answer to British proposals of coercion towards Turkey, conveyed Russia's intentions in his warning note to the Salisbury Government, and England, who in 1878 had rivetted the Turkish yoke on the necks of the Armenians, to use the words of an eminent British authority on Turkish affairs, "wrung her hands and submitted."[6]

The same authority tells us that the *coup de grace* to the intervention of the Concert of Europe in Armenian affairs was given by Prince Bismarck, "who in 1883 intimated to the British Government, in terms of cynical frankness and force, that Germany cared nothing about the matter, and that it had better be allowed to drop."

Thus the Concert of Europe, under whose aegis the aspiring Armenians foolishly and fondly hoped to recover National Autonomy, became the cause of dealing out to the struggling nation, not security from Turkish oppression, but instead fire, famine and slaughter, a slaughter to which were added devilish ingenuity of torture, and the loathsome horrors of Turkish prisons. If before the Treaty of Berlin the Armenians had suffered from various phases of Turkish oppression, they had at least not been pursued with the relentless fury that followed, until the soil of the fatherland was soaked, and reeked and steamed with the life-blood of its slaughtered sons and

---

[5] Commenting on the effect on Abdul Hamid of the indignation aroused in England over the massacres, Mr. James Bryce writes, "The indignation expressed in England exasperated him; he passed from fear to fury, and back again to fear; and went so far as to beg, and obtain, the friendly offices of the Pope, who, through the Government of Spain, asked the British Government not to press too hardly upon the Sultan with regard to the Armenians."—Note to 2nd printing.

[6] "Transcaucasia and Ararat: Twenty Years of the Armenian Question."—James Bryce. Note to 2nd printing.

daughters; until women and children were done to their death under the most hideous and revolting circumstances, and tender youths and cultured men of letters rotted in Turkish dungeons.

England, with her uneasy conscience, continued spasmodic efforts in the shape of paper remonstrances, from time to time she rallied the other powers who were signatories to the Treaty of Berlin and by means of Ambassadorial Identical Notes and Collective Notes sought to terminate the horrors that were stirring public feeling at home; but Abdul Hamid, fully cognizant of the jealousies and rivalries of the Powers, and knowing himself secure thereby, laughed in his sleeve at all the paper remonstrances.

No action was taken by the Cabinets of Europe to leash the tiger sitting on the Ottoman throne. The lust of blood and the lust of plunder of "le Sultan Rouge," combined with the greed of his satellites, were allowed to be gratified to the full on a helpless and hapless people, whilst Europe looked on.

The character of Abdul Hamid has been well summed up in the testimony of a writer having opportunities of intimate acquaintance with him.

"Il voit dans son peuple un vil troupeau qu'il peut dévorer sans pitié, et à qui, comme le lion de la Fable, il fait beaucoup d'honneur en daignant le croquer."[7]

---

[7] "Abdul Hamid Intime," Georges Dorys. In the Preface by Pierre Guillard to the same book, there occurs the following passage: "Gladstone dénonça le Grand Assassin; M. Albert Vandal flétrit le Sultan Rouge; M. Anatole France fit trembler dans l'antre de Yildiz le Despote fou d'épouvante et d'autres le traitèrent de Bête Rouge et de Sultan blême.

"Cependant aucun de ces termes excessifs en apparence n'est encore satisfaisant et n'exprime en toute son horreur le caractère d'un être à face humaine, tel, disait récemment un haut exilé ottoman, qu'il

When to these significant words, we add the following by the same author:—

"De ce qu'Abdul Hamid n'est pas bon musulman, il ne faudrait pas conclure qu'il aime les Chrétiens; il les déteste, au contraire, et emploie fréquemment le mot *giaour* pour désigner un infidèle ou insulter un musulman."

We have the explanation of the Armenian massacres; especially as that unfortunate people had become by Article 61 of the Treaty of Berlin, subjects of the paper remonstrances of the Powers of Europe, and thereby also objects of the tyrant's vengeance.

GENERAL TER GOUKASSOFF

Relieved the beleaguered Russian garrison at Bayazid during the Russo-Turkish war of 1877, captured the fortress; and otherwise distinguished himself during the war.

The other Armenian General who distinguished himself during the Russo-Turkish war was General Lazaroff.

---

n'en existe point de semblable, qu'il n'en a jamais existé de pareil et que selon toute probabilité, il n'en pourra dans l'avenir exister un second. Les conquérants assyriens qui se vantent dans des inscriptions lapidaires d'avoir exterminé les peuples rebelles et tendu de peaux écorchées les murailles des villes prises, Néron, Caligula, Timour, Gengiz Khan, les inquisiteurs catholiques et les tortionnaires chinois, aucun tueur d'hommes n'égala Abdul-Hamid."—Note to 2nd printing.

That the Armenians should be constantly appealing to the Power that had pledged itself for their protection, and that the same Power should be constantly rallying the others, and making Ambassadorial demonstrations, was enough to rouse the vilest passions of a nature in which no feelings except vile passions existed.

Of all sins in this world, perhaps the sin of foolishness receives the severest punishment, and of all crimes, the crime of failure meets with the heaviest doom. For their foolishness in trusting in European protection and hoping for European intervention the unfortunate Armenians paid with rivers of their own blood, and for their crime of failure they were made to wallow in that blood. The darkest pages of their history have been written in the closing years of the nineteenth, and the early years of the twentieth century; never since the loss of their independence, nine centuries ago, had they hoped for so much, and never had they paid so dearly for their folly.

If they had carefully laid to heart the whole history of Europe's intercourse with Asia, beginning with the conquests of the Macedonian Alexander, they would have read in the light of sober judgement, self-interest, and self-interest only written on every line and page, but they committed the folly of hoping that for their sakes the history of the world, which means in other words the history of human selfishness, was going to be reversed; and they forgot what was more important than all, that Europe had nothing to gain by their emancipation. There is only one explanation for their folly. It is a peculiarity of human nature that the troubles we have been bearing with more or less patience, become unbearable when once hopes of deliverance from them are awakened. Article 61 of the Treaty of Berlin awakened hopes that proved bitterer in the eating than Dead Sea fruit. It aroused towards the Armenians the diabolical animosity of the human fiend who held sovereignty over them.

Hunted like wild beasts, killed like rats and flies, out of the depths of its agony and its martyrdom, the nation has still contrived to rear its head and live; for it was as it is now, the industrious, energetic, self-respecting element in the Turkish Empire, with a virile life in its loins and sinews, that centuries of oppression culminating in the unspeakable horrors of a thirty years' martyrdom has failed to exterminate.

As for the Treaty of Berlin—It has done its work.

THE ARMENIAN MASSACRES AND THE TURKISH CONSTITUTION

The Turkish Constitution came with a bound that shook the equanimity of Europe. To the anxious and jealously watching eyes of Europe the "sick man in her midst" was at last becoming moribund. His recovery was as startling as unexpected. Europe had not correctly gauged the latent forces within the Turkish Empire, neither had she correctly estimated the far-reaching astuteness of the tyrant on the throne.

Assailed by enemies from without and within, feeling the foundation of his throne crumbling, Abdul Hamid, arch murderer and assassin, performed his own *auto da fé*, and rose from his ashes a constitutional sovereign. The obduracy of the merciless tyrant melted like wax before the approach of personal danger, and the act was necessary to save himself.

Hopes rose high at such a magnificent *coup d'état* of the revolutionaries. Young Turks and Armenians fell on each other's necks, embraced, and mingled their tears of joy together. Leaders of the Turkish Constitution proclaimed in public speeches that the Turks owed the deepest debt of gratitude to the Armenians who had been the initiators of their struggle for Freedom, and in the Armenian graveyard at Constantinople Turks held a memorial service and kissed the graves of the Armenian dead, whom they called "the martyrs whose blood had been shed for Turkish freedom."

At the banquet given by Abdul Hamid to the Delegates of the Turkish Parliament, the Armenian Delegates alone refused to attend, declining to be the guest of the man responsible for the murder of hundreds of thousands of their countrymen.

The Armenian revolutionaries had stood behind the Young Turk party and joined hands with them; already the nation at large imagined itself breathing the air of Freedom, and already in anticipation drank in deep draughts of the air of Liberty.

The awakening came all too quickly. In spite of the Constitution the machinations of Abdul Hamid and his palace clique could find fruitful ground among a fanatical populace to whom the Padishah was not only the Lord's anointed but the Lord's appointed, the delegate of the Prophet on whom his sacred mantle had fallen; added to this the incentive of pecuniary rewards to a brutal soldiery and the lust of plunder, and once more the horrors of massacres were let loose on the Armenians. There followed sacked and burning villages, plundered and devastated homes, an unarmed population put to the sword, and as in every case, cruelties of the most hideous and ferocious nature perpetrated on women and children.

In the whole long story of the massacres, courage to face their oppressors has never been found wanting on the part of the Armenians. It is on record that the women of a whole mountain village surprised by Turkish soldiers, in the absence of the men, fought and resisted to the last gasp, and finally, to escape the clutches of the brutal soldiery, committed suicide with their children by precipitating themselves from their mountain cliffs. A nation which could produce such women, and which has had the simple courage to die for its faith, as no Christian people has died before, is not wanting in brave men, but no amount of bravery and heroism can save an unarmed population from being mowed down by soldiery equipped with modern instruments of carnage and slaughter.

The horrors of Adana coming on the heels of a Constitution they had aided, and from which they had hoped so much, presages grave fears for the Armenians.

No one doubts that a great forward movement is reaching its

culminating point in the destiny of Asia. The West has learnt its all of religion (the moral and guiding principle of mankind) from the East, and now the East would fain learn the law of restraint and the law of freedom (the protecting principles of mankind) from the West. Inspired by this feeling the liberal Turks decidedly mean well, and they are animated with a sincere desire to ensure peace and security of life and property for the heterogeneous peoples under the Turkish sway, but they themselves have had to contend and still have to contend with a fanatical populace.

To the Mahommedan world at large the Caliph of Islam is the envoy of God, the sacredness of whose person must be inviolate. Abdul Hamid, the astute politician, knew that the security of his sovereignty depended on his Caliphal rights, and his main policy during the long period of his execrable reign had been directed towards preserving and asserting the same; thus we can see how his dethronement, which the liberal Turks would gladly have accomplished simultaneously with the inauguration of the Constitution, had to be deferred to a later period, and how it was necessary for the Sheik ul Islam to pronounce the Caliph a traitor to his sacred trust, a violator of the holy law of the Prophet, before his dethronement could be dared or accomplished.

The Christian Armenians in Turkey live in the midst of the followers of a hostile religion, with no power or force behind them which makes for protection. Who does not know that the great numerical preponderance of Hinduism keeps the balance of power in India, and restrains bloody religious hostilities; and when we review the whole religious history of Christian Europe, and that terribly long roll of crimes committed in the name of Him who expounded His religion with the parable of the Good Samaritan, and the precept of loving one's neighbour as one's self, we cannot feel surprise at the fanatical outbursts of the followers of Mahommed, the founder of a religion whose doctrines certainly fall short of the humane principles inculcated by the Founder of Christianity. If authentic historical facts prove to us that horrible and atrocious cruelties have been perpetrated by Christian nations, not only on other religionists, but on fellow Christians of different denominations, how then can we expect better things from the Turk unless some power or force restrain him?

Christianity has now partly emancipated herself from the ferocities which darkened and poured the red stream of blood on her white banner: but to the Mahommedan world at large, religion is still the powder magazine which a spark can ignite.

"Better the Czar than the Sultan, but better any form of national autonomy than either Czar or Sultan" has been the principle which has animated the Armenians, and the goal towards which they have been striving for thirty years.

National Autonomy has been the dream of the Armenians in Turkey, but it is well to consider if such a dream has any possibility of realization. Bulgaria declared her independence, and Austria annexed Bosnia and Herzegovina, but these reductions of Turkish power were accomplished by the force that stood behind them. Have the Armenians any such force which could accomplish their deliverance? Have they an organized army at their command? Are they equipped with all the necessary weapons of modern warfare? are questions it is well for the nation to ask before it makes itself a target for Turkish bullets.

On the other hand is it likely that the Turks will willingly give the Armenians independence? To do so would mean that they should themselves dismember their own Empire, and when we see Christian Governments actuated in their foreign policy by the supremest selfishness; Christian Governments striving tooth and nail in their own self interest to keep possessions which are lawfully not their own, then why in the name of common sense should we expect such extraordinary magnanimity, or such super-nobility from the Turk.

Armenia stands in the unhappy position of being divided between Russia and Turkey (if we except Persia, which does not count for much since 1827). It is evident that even the Czar Liberator, if he had been allowed to carry out his humanitarian endeavours, would have liberated Armenia from Turkey, not to give her independence but to make her into a Russian possession, for to have given Turkish Armenia independence would have been tantamount to fostering the spirit of independence in those provinces of Armenia which had already passed under Russian rule.

It is well known that the Emperor Alexander II was guided and influenced by the liberal principles of Loris Melikoff (or properly Melikian according to the Armenian termination of his name). Melikian enjoyed the personal friendship of the Czar, and the successful victor of Kars was rewarded by his august master with the office of Prime Minister. The policy of Melikian made for the Russofication of Armenia, and while it is not possible that he loved Russia more than he loved his own country, it is rather more than probable that he saw in the Russofication of his nation the only way of saving its people.

With the death of Alexander II Melikian's star passed out of the horizon of Russian ministership; his liberal principles were not acceptable to Alexander III, and the policy of Russia towards the Armenians underwent a decided change.

Since the disastrous war with Japan the policy of Russia towards the Armenians has undergone another change. In the years preceding the war, the reigning autocrat had pursued the policy of his father to an even greater degree of repression. Not only had national schools and theatres been closed in Russian

Armenia and newspapers suspended, but the Czar went still further, and confiscated the lands and the wealth of the Armenian church.

The late Armenian Catholicos Mukertich Khirimian (one of the delegates sent to the Congress of Berlin by the Patriarch Nerses), to whom his own people had given the beloved appellation of "Hairik" (little father) had by his noble life of self-sacrifice, his unceasing labours for the cause of the people, and his remarkable individuality, come to be regarded as a sort of holy man. There in the Cathedral of Etchmiatzin, under the venerable dome where for seventeen hundred years the successors of Gregore Loosavoritch (Gregory the Illuminator) had each in his turn held sway, and worshipped on the spot where the vision of Christ the Lord had descended, there before the altar of Christ, had Hairik the holy man lifted up his voice and cursed—cursed the Czar; and cursed Russia—Pious Russia with its pious Czar at its head shuddered, and the astounding reverses in the war with Japan that followed were attributed to Khirimian's curse.

Russia in Expiation made Reparation: the ban on schools, theatres and newspapers was removed, the church lands and the church wealth were restored, and the Czar of all the Russias in a friendly note to the Armenian Catholicos assured him of the Imperial friendship, and the Imperial solicitude for the welfare of his people.

The return from exile of the Patriarch Ezmerlian to Constantinople, was quickly followed by his nomination to the See of Etchmiatzin, left vacant by the death of his predecessor, and now we hear of the Catholicos appealing to the Russian Government to take over the protectorate of Armenia from Turkey. Ezmerlian knows Turkey, he has been in close touch with the liberal Turks, and he knows the Turkish nation as a whole; he knows also that the present and immediate future of Russia is dark in the gloom of autocratic Czardom, and a man of his intellectual attainments and liberal principles can have no sympathy with absolutism. The appeal therefore of the Catholicos Ezmerlian (the Iron Patriarch as he is familiarly known) must be read as a premonition, that not only has all hope of wresting national autonomy from Turkey died in his resolute heart, but also that he entertains grave fears of the possibility of the horrors of Adana being repeated.

MUCKERTICH KHIRIMIAN

(Late Catholicos and Supreme Patriarch of Etchmiatzin. Author and Poet).

Russia may go on massacring Jews until Russians have left off being fanatical devils, and learned to be human, but however much she may pursue the policy of suppressing nationalism, however much she may seek to absorb the nation into herself, she has stopped at slaughter as far as Armenians are concerned. In his appeal to Russia, the Catholicos can be actuated by no other motive except the one motive of safe-guarding the people, of whom he is the acknowledged head.

A man of high character and a dauntless patriot, known to his people under the beloved appellation of "Hairik" (little father). He was one of the delegates sent by the Patriarch Nerses to the Congress of Berlin in 1878. He worked for the cause of the people during his whole life, and died, worn out with heartbreaking disappointments; his dying words were, "We must not despair."

In an article entitled "The Church of Ararat" by Henry W. Nevinson in Harper's Monthly Magazine of April, 1908 there is given the following interesting account of the late Catholicos.

> The old man was sitting up in bed, a gray rug neatly spread over him for counterpane. There was something childlike and appealing in his position, as there always is about a sick man lying in bed in the daytime. One felt a little brutal standing beside him, dressed, and well, and tingling from the cold outside. It was a time for soothing hands and motherly care to put this baby of fourscore years to rest. But his mother was long ago forgotten: even his wife had been dead for half a century; and his only nurse was a stalwart black-bearded bishop of middle age.
>
> It was a long, low room, pleasant in its austerity. The whitewashed walls, the bare floor, the absence of all ornament, told of a clean and devoted mind. The windows looked upon a courtyard, silent but for the murmur and fluttering of pigeons. The old man's hands lay quiet on the blanket, white, and wasted almost to the bone. The nightgown hid a form so thin it hardly made a ripple under the clothes. Through the white and shrunken face every lineament of the future skull was already visible; but on each side of the thin nose, hooked like a round bow, a great brown eye revealed the inward spirit's intelligence and zeal unquenched. On his head was a close-fitting cap of purple velvet.

Thus, near the end of last December, one of a century's greatest men—Mgrditch Khrimian, Katholikos of the Armenian Church, and soul of the Armenian people—slowly approaching to death, lay in the ancient monastery called Etchmiatzin, or "The Only-Begotten is Descended." From the window of a neighboring room he might have looked across the frost bound plain of the Araxes, where the vines were now all cut close and buried for the winter. Beyond the plain stood a dark mass of whirling snow and hurricane that hid the cone of Ararat. And just beyond Ararat lies Lake Van, last puddle of the Deluge. On the shore of that lake, eighty-seven years ago, Khrimian was born. In 1820 the Turkish Empire was still undiminished by sea or land; the Sultan still counted as one of the formidable Powers of Europe. It was four years before Byron set out to deliver Greece from his tyranny, and established for England a reputation as the generous champion of freedom—a reputation which still rather pathetically survives throughout the Near East. Long and stormy had been the life upon which the Katholikos now looked back, but not unhappy, for from first to last it had been inspired by one absorbing and unselfish aim—the freedom and regeneration of his people. It is true he had failed.

From his earliest years, when he had witnessed the terrors of Turkish oppression in the homes of Armenians round Ararat, he was possessed by the spirit of nationality—such a spirit as only kindles in oppressed races, but dies away into easygoing tolerance among the prosperous and contented of the world. He began as a poet, wandering far and wide through the Turkish, Persian, and Russian sections of Armenia, visiting Constantinople and Jerusalem, and recalling to his people by his poems the scenes and glories of their national history. Entering the monastic order after his wife's death, he devoted himself to the building of schools, which he generously threw open to Kurds, the hereditary assassins of Armenians. For many years, while Europe was occupied with Crimean wars, Austrian wars, or French and German wars, we see him ceaselessly journeying from Van to Constantinople and through the cities of Asia, unyielding in the contest, though continually defeated, his schools burned, his printing-presses broken up, his sacred emblems of the Host hung in mockery round the necks of dogs. When elected Armenian patriarch of Constantinople (1869), he was driven from his office after four years.

But the cup of Turkish iniquity was filling. The pitiless slaughter of Bulgarians and Armenians alike was more than even the European Powers could stand. With varied motives, Russia sent her armies to fight their way to the walls of Constantinople, and Khrimian found himself summoned to plead his people's cause before the Congress of Berlin. Though he speaks no language but Armenian and Turkish, he visited all the great courts of Europe beforehand, urging them to create an autonomous neutral state for Armenia, as they had done with success for the Lebanon. In London he became acquainted with Gladstone; but Gladstone was then only the blazing firebrand which had kindled the heart of England, and, in the Congress itself Khrimian could gain nothing for his people beyond the promises of Article 61, pledging the Powers, and especially England, to hold the Kurds in check and enforce Turkey's definite reforms. It is needless to say that none of these promises and pledges were observed. Beaconsfield returned to London amid shouts of "Peace with Honor," and Armenia was left to stew.

So it went on. Detained in Constantinople as prisoner, banished to Jerusalem for rebellion, and finally chosen Katholikos, or head of his Church and race, by his own people, he maintained the hopeless contest. Year by year the woe increased, till by the last incalculable crime (1894-1896), the Armenians were slaughtered like sheep from the Bosporus to Lake Van, and the lowest estimate counted the murdered dead at 100,000. Gladstone made the last great speech of his heroic life. England attempted some kind of protest. But rather than join the Liberal demand for action, Lord Rosebery left his party for private leisure, and Russia, France, and Germany combined to secure immunity for the "great assassin." It was the lowest point of Europe's shame.

Blow followed blow. Hardly had the remnant of the Armenian people escaped from massacre when their Church fell under the brutal domination of Russia. Plehve ordained its destruction, and Golitzin was sent to Tiflis as governor-general to carry it out. Church property to the value of £6,000,000 was seized by violence, the Katholikos resolutely refusing to give up the keys of the safe where the title deeds were kept (June, 1903). For two years the Russian officials played with the revenues, retaining eighty per cent. for their own advantage. But in the mean time assassination had rid the earth of Plehve, and the overwhelming defeats of Russia in Manchuria were attributed to the Armenian curse. Grudgingly the Church property was restored, in utter chaos, and for the moment it is Russia's policy to favor the Armenians as a balance against the Georgians, whom the St. Petersburg government is now determined to destroy.

Such was the past upon which the worn old man, stretched on his monastic bed, looked back that winter's morning. Singleness of aim has its reward in spiritual peace, but of the future he was not hopeful. He no longer even contemplated an autonomous Armenia, either on Turkish territory or on Russian. On the Russian side of the frontier the Armenian villages were too scattered, too much interspersed with Georgians and Tartars, to allow of autonomy. On the Turkish side, he thought, massacre and exile had now left too few of the race to form any kind of community. Indeed, for the last twelve years the Armenian villagers have been crawling over the foot of Ararat by thousands a year to escape the Kurds, and every morning they come and stand in fresh groups of pink and blue rags outside the monastery door where the head of their Church and race lies dying. They stand there in mute appeal, as I saw them, possessing nothing in the world but the variegated tatters that cover them, and their faith in their Katholikos. Slowly they are drafted away into Tiflis, Baku, or their Caucasian villages, but nowhere are they welcomed.

Some of the bishops and monks, who form a council round their chief, still look for Europe's interference, and trust that the solemn pledges taken by England and other Powers at Berlin may be fulfilled. The Bishop of Erivan, for instance, still labors for the appointment of a Christian governor over the district marked by the ill-omened names of Van, Bitlis, and Erzeroum. I also found that even among the Georgians there was a large party willing to concede all the frontier district from Erivan to Kars, where Armenian villages are thickest, as an autonomous Armenian province, in the happy day when the Caucasus wins federal autonomy. But the majority of the Armenian clergy, who hitherto have led the people, are beginning to acquiesce in the hopelessness of political change, and are now limiting their efforts to education and industries. One cannot yet say how far their influence may be surpassed in the growing revolutionary parties of "The Bell" and "The Flag." Of these, the Social Democratic "Bell" follows the usual impracticable and pedantic creed of St. Marx. The "Flag," or party of Nationalist Democrats, is at present dominant, and at a great assembly held in Erivan last August (1906) they adopted a programme of land nationalization, universal suffrage and education, an eight-hour day, and the control of the Church property by elected laymen. If the Russian revolution makes good progress, they will naturally unite with the Georgian Federalists, on whom the best hopes of the country are set.

Whatever may be the political future of the Armenians, they seem likely to survive for many generations yet as a race, held together by language and religion. Except the Jews, there is, I think, no parallel to such a survival. It is a thousand years since they could be called a powerful nation. For almost as long they have possessed no independent country of their own. For six hundred years their ancient capital city of Ani has stood a splendid but empty ruin in the desert between Kars and the great mountain of Alagöz, which confronts Ararat, with nearly equal height. They have been rent asunder and tormented by Persians, Turks, Tartars, and Russians in turn. Even their religion is not nationalistic or distinctly separate from other forms of religion, like the Jewish. Except for metaphysical shades of difference, hardly comprehensible to the modern world, there is little to distinguish it from the orthodox Christianity of the Near East. Yet, through innumerable disasters and attempts at extermination, the race persists, like the Jews, with astonishing vitality, unmistakable in characteristics which may not be exactly heroic, but lead to a certain material success. After all, it is only in harassed and persecuted nationalities that true patriotism ever survives.

MATTHEVOSE EZMERLIAN

Catholicos and Supreme Patriarch of Etchmiatzin. A man of high character and great ability, also a distinguished linguist. As Patriarch of Constantinople he was familiarly known as the "Iron Patriarch." Banished by the Hamidian Government, he returned from exile in 1908 and was shortly after elected Catholicos of Etchmiatzin.

The Armenian Catholicos is not infallible like the Pope. He is elected by the nation, but his appointment is subject to the sanction of the Czar.

THE ARMENIAN MASSACRES AND THE ARMENIAN PEOPLE

During a period extending over thirty years the civilized world has heard of Turkish Massacres of Armenians. Massacres of a nature so ferocious and diabolical, so hideous and revolting, that no pen could adequately describe their horrors.

Writing in 1896, Mr. James Bryce, in his supplementary chapter to the 4th edition of his book "Transcaucasia and Ararat" makes the following grave comment:—

"Twenty years is a short space in the life of a nation. But these twenty years have been filled with sufferings for the Armenian Christians greater than their ancestors had to endure during the eight centuries that have passed since the first Turkish Conquest of Armenia. They have been years of misery, slaughter, martyrdom, agony, despair."

And the years that have followed from 1896 to 1909 have had the same tale of woe to unfold; a tale of horrors such as have never been surpassed in the history of nations.

The opinion of the Turkish Pasha, "The way to get rid of the Armenian Question, is to get rid of the Armenians" was followed by "le Sultan Rouge," and that the monster and assassin who sat on the Turkish throne from 1876 to 1909 was not able to accomplish this policy to the bitter end of complete extermination, was no doubt due to the grit and stubborn endurance of the victims.

A Turkish writer has made the remark, "There are Armenians, but there is no Armenia." This assertion would be true if meant in a political sense only, for of all civilized races on earth, Armenians are politically one of the most forlorn, but the country has not been wiped off the map. It still occupies the geographical place it has held since history has been written. The land of the Euphrates and Tigris, that Araxes valley, where, as simple and primitive Armenians will to this day assert in unshaken belief, God made man in His own image, and the country round the base of Ararat, where the generations of men once more began to people the earth.

Once the land of Ararat was an independent kingdom until the tide of victory rolled over it and conquered its independence. Hemmed round by three Great Empires, Russian, Turkish and Persian, the unfortunate geographical position of the country became the cause of its people's ruin.

It is of bitter interest to Armenians to know that Ararat is the point where the three Empires, Russian, Turkish and Persian, meet, whilst the children of the land of Ararat have passed under the sovereignties of Czar, Sultan and Shah. Thus it may be true that there is no Armenia in the political sense of the word, but if Armenia has lost her independence, the Armenian people have survived.

The Author of "Transcaucasia and Ararat" thus writes of them:—

"The Armenians are an extraordinary people, with a tenacity of national life scarcely inferior to that of the Jews."

The remark is true. There are two nations of antiquity who notwithstanding unremitting persecutions, and centuries of loss of independence, have survived their contemporary nations; their fortunes have run on parallel lines, though their national characteristics have been different in some respects. Together with his other avocations, the Armenian is mountaineer, soldier, labourer, agriculturist, while the Jew is purely a dweller in cities; but the same virility of life, the same mental and physical strength have sustained both. The sons of Heber, great grandson of Shem, have however become wise in their generation, the Jew is now more American than the American, more British than the British, more French than the French, more German than the German. Not so the sons of Haik, great grandson of Japhet, for with the same determined obstinacy with which he has clung to his faith, the Armenian clings to his nationality. He has known how to resist Russian endeavours of absorption, and Turkish systems of extermination. When he gives up his nationality, it will be the story of the hunted animal brought to its last gasp.

The Armenians have been called "the most determined of Christians," a remark the truth of which has been borne out by their unequalled martyrdom for their faith; and yet it may truly be said that in no Christian Church is the lay element more strong than it is in the Armenian Church. Conscious of this freedom, Armenians are surprised to read assertions made by some writers, about "the gross superstitions" of their Church, which they on their part regard as the happy medium between Protestantism and Roman Catholicism. Surrounded with pomp and splendour, and a show of outward ceremonies, which the average Armenian regards as no more than mere adjuncts to gratify and impress the sensibilities, the Liturgy of the Armenian Church, in its grandeur and pathos, appeals to the heart of the Armenian people, as no other form of worship can; it is the reason, as has truly been said of them, that "they carry their religion with them wherever they go."

The Armenians have also been called "the interpreters between the East and the West." There is no doubt a certain adaptability which is a national characteristic; and as language is the vehicle of comprehension, their talent for acquiring languages helps to bring them into touch with Eastern and Western peoples; but the main truth of the observation lies in the fact, that being born Asiatics, and living for the most part in the midst of Asiatic surroundings, they fall into the ways of Asiatic life; they understand Asiatics better, and know how to sympathise with them; whilst on the other hand, their religion is the religion which has moulded the thought of the West, and consequently also the religion that has moulded the thought of a people who were the earliest Christians.

The main point of social difference between them and other Asiatic nations, lies in the exalted position occupied by their women, and this point of difference may be traced to that one cause or influence, which has exalted the position of women in the West, the doctrines of Jesus of Nazareth. This point of difference in social life, together with the difference of religion, has always kept them separate from Persian and Turk.

Private and trustworthy information to hand brings the news that the ex Sultan Abdul Hamid, aware of his impending dethronement, desired to bring about a general massacre of Christians in Constantinople, beginning with the foreign Embassies downwards. "I must be the last Padishah, even though Turkey perish," was Abdul's frantic appeal to his satellites, but his minions, not daring to venture on so dangerous an undertaking, planned the massacres to begin at the village of Adana, inhabited by the unfortunate Armenians. It was a safe plan, since the Armenians had no battleships to turn their guns upon Constantinople, and by the bombardment of the capital, to seek revenge for the murder of their countrymen.

A massacre so wanton as that of Adana, can only find its counterpart in the other Turkish massacres of Armenians which preceded it.

"Abdul the Damned" has been dethroned, but he has not been executed, and so long as he continues to draw breath, as long is there danger for the Armenians.

We hear of the Mahommedans in India cabling their petition to the new Turkish Government to spare the life of the ex-Padishah and the ex-Caliph of Islam; the erstwhile "God's shadow on earth" and the erstwhile "God's envoy on earth" the sacredness of whose person should be inviolate. In this demonstration of the Indian Mahommedans, we can read the epistle of Mahommedan thought, and feel the pulse of Mahommedan feeling all over the Sunni Moslem world.

Although intensely mercenary, Abdul Hamid however not only never grudged the gold which helped to accomplish the Armenian massacres, but he used it largely in douceurs which purchased silence or false representations of his diabolical acts, and it was by means of such douceurs that he went farther than seducing merely his own subjects.

"Mais l'oeuvre de l'impérial corrupteur a dépassé les limites de son Palais et de ses États, N'a-t-il pas, en effet, étouffé sous des baillons dorés la voix d'importants organes de la presse européenne? N'a-t-il pas acheté à l'étranger des politiciens et même des diplomates?

"Saïd Pacha ayant recherché ce qu'en six mois les massacres d'Arménie avaient coûté au Trésor turc, en allocations à certains journaux européens, a établi le compte approximatif suivant: 640 décorations, et 235,000 Livres Turques (près de cinq millions et demi)!"[8]

It needs not be added that no one who knows the truth of Turkish affairs, doubts the truth of this impeachment.

"But whatever the future may bring, the past is past, and will one day fall to be judged. And of the judgement of posterity there can be little doubt."

In these memorable words, Mr. James Bryce in the supplementary chapter of his book "Transcaucasia and Ararat" concludes his criticism on what he calls "the fatal action followed by the fatal inaction of the European Powers."

---

[8] "Abdul Hamid Intime," Georges Dorys.—Note to 2nd printing.

It is true. As surely as the world revolves on her own axis, and as day succeeds night, so surely History will record and Posterity will judge. But what compensation to the Armenians? What compensation for the rivers of blood that have inundated their land? What atonement for the hideous past? What relief for the present? What hope for the future?

THE ARMENIAN MASSACRES AND THE FUTURE OF THE ARMENIANS

The above is a subject for profound meditation for the Armenian people; it has therefore naturally for me occupied much deep thought.

National Autonomy has been the dream of the Armenians; a dream which through centuries of oppression and years of slaughter, the nation has been striving and struggling to realize. The oldest of historical nations, we have held to our nationality, language and religion; we have struggled and striven, and though billows of affliction have swept over us, we have not allowed ourselves to be engulfed. "Love is stronger than Death" and truly the Armenian has loved his nationality with a steadfastness and tenacity that has conquered death.

Steady, stubborn grit, combined with a remarkable natural intelligence have been characteristics of the race, and have kept us alive in spite of national adversities, such as no other nation could have suffered and survived.

But our position is an acutely unhappy and an acutely unfortunate one. Our misfortunes began with the physical geography of our country. Surrounded by three great empires, our kingdom was strangled by the overwhelming pressure, and to-day our country is divided up between Russia, Turkey and Persia. For this reason we have been a great deal more unfortunate than the Balkan States, and now if there were any possible chance of wresting autonomy for Turkish Armenia from Turkey, Russia fearing the spread of the same spirit in her own provinces, would assuredly not only frown on such an attempt but use all the means in her power to crush it.

There is also a stern fact which a people so politically helpless and forlorn as ourselves must ever bear in mind, namely, that we live in an intensely selfish and intensely grasping world; no prating the pretty nonsense of Western Civilization, or Western Humanity, or Western Christianity can alter that stern hard fact as it stands, and as it has stood since the history of our world has been written.

Indeed, nineteenth century civilization, which has made the world of commerce acutely grasping, has also made the world of Politics unscrupulously selfish.

However much it may clothe itself in the garment of fair speech, what we call "Politics" is actually made up of that one devouring, absorbing, grasping element—Selfishness. "The friends of to-day may be enemies to-morrow" is more truly spoken in the domain of Politics than anywhere else.

Let the Armenians take a lesson not only from the Turkish massacres, but from the attitude of Europe towards those massacres? Let them look back on the past, and remember how they have been trampled under the merciless foot of Political Selfishness, and then left to welter in their gore.

Who doubts, who can gainsay, that by so much as the lifting up of a finger the Powers of Europe could have stopped those massacres? Was that finger ever lifted up, however, all through the long years of "slaughter, martyrdom, agony, despair" to save our helpless people from butcheries so enormous, so hideous, so appalling that no pen could portray the horrible realities? Had the Turkish bonds been in jeopardy, Constantinople harbour would have witnessed the battleships of the Powers of Europe discharging their cannon on the capital of the Turkish Empire, but a hundred thousand or five hundred thousand Armenians, more or less, mangled and butchered to death, or fleeing from their sacked and burning villages to die of cold and starvation in their mountain passes, could not rouse action on the part of

Europe, even though the Concert of Europe had been instrumental in their destruction.

I do not write with a desire to indulge in recriminations, since vain recriminations will not bear profitable fruit; but I write with the object of impressing on my countrymen to remember, always to remember, the lessons written on the pages of a past that should never be forgotten by us.

In his book "Our Responsibilities for Turkey" the late Duke of Argyll quotes from the famous despatch of a British Ambassador to Turkey, the date being given as September 4, 1876. The despatch proceeds thus:—

"To the accusation of being a blind partisan of the Turks I will only answer that my conduct here has never been guided by any sentimental affection for them, but by a firm determination to uphold the interests of Great Britain to the utmost of my power; and that those interests are deeply engaged in preventing the disruption of the Turkish Empire is a conviction which I share in common with the most eminent statesmen who have directed our foreign policy, but which appears now to be abandoned by shallow politicians or persons who have allowed their feelings of revolted humanity to make them forget the capital interests involved in the question.

"We may and must feel indignant at the needless and monstrous severity with which the Bulgarian insurrection was put down; *but the necessity which exists for England to prevent changes from occurring here which would be most detrimental to ourselves is not affected by the question whether it was 10,000 or 20,000 persons who perished in the suppression.*

"We have been upholding what we know to be a semi-civilized nation, liable under certain circumstances to be carried into fearful excesses; but the fact of this having just now been strikingly brought home to us all cannot be a sufficient reason for abandoning a policy which is the only one that can be followed with due regard to our interest."

I quote this famous despatch merely to point out that "due regard to our interest" was carefully followed out in the Past by the Powers of Europe, and that "due regard to our interest" will be just as carefully followed out in the Present and in the Future.

From the Turk and Persian, the Armenian must ever remain separate, as he has through centuries, though living in the midst of them, remained separate. The gulf that divides the one nation from the other two, the wall of iron that rises between them is the position of woman. The Armenian has accepted wholeheartedly the position in which woman has been placed by the Great Founder of his faith. For seventeen hundred years unremittingly since Christianity was revived in Armenia by Gregory the Illuminator, the Christian law with regard to the position of woman has moulded the thought of the nation, it has left its impress on the nation, and it is this vital and essential difference between the law of Mahommed and the law of Christ that like a two-edged sword has cleaved apart Christian Armenian from Moslem Turk and Persian.

If "East is East, and West is West" it is on account of the social plane on which woman stands, a social plane that is never so degraded in any corner of Asia, as it is in the countries where the law of Mahommed governs.

The Armenians in Asiatic Turkey are scattered and dispersed among Turks and other antagonistic races; they are without any military force or organization to wrest autonomy from the military and governing power. That Europe should aid their endeavours, or that Turkey should make them a free gift of autonomy, are both of them absolutely out of the question. Then what remains for us?

To hold to our own nationality and to be subject—Subject to

Russia, subject to Turkey, subject to Persia—What shall it profit us? What will it profit? What doth it profit us? Our strong, clever, energetic men, our beautiful, intelligent women, when neither chance nor opportunity can enable our finest and best to reach the higher rungs of the world's ladder, and when as a subject people we must ever remain hewers of wood and drawers of water, even our Aivasowskis and our Melikoffs have been known to the world as Russians, not as Armenians. Have we a chance of bursting the fetters? Have we strength to break the chains? Can we reach the goal toward which, bleeding and torn, we have been striving, and still are striving? These are questions which we must ask ourselves; looking them soberly in the face.

But this is not enough: if we must persist in holding to our nationality, we must look into ourselves, we must search out and probe our national failings and our national weaknesses, and find out in what essential characteristics we are wanting as a nation, and so build up national character. Let us weigh ourselves in the balance, and supply what in us is found wanting.

In the period of less than a decade a Great Power has risen in the Orient. The people of a small island empire with an empty Treasury have beaten successfully and disastrously a colossal empire of whom the Powers of Europe had stood in awe, and against whom not one had ventured single-handed to engage.

On the field the ever victorious army of little Japan undermined Russia's stronghold, and succeeded in driving back and ever driving back the ever defeated and ever retreating army of colossal Russia. At sea the ever victorious Japanese Fleet succeeded in completely annihilating the Russian Fleet. It was war such as the world had never yet seen. The secret of such astounding successes should be investigated, and here I beg leave to quote from one of a series of articles in which I gave view to my opinions during the Russo-Japanese War. "Japan may be likened to the bundle of faggots in the fable firmly tied together; one faggot of larger dimensions in the centre, the sovereign round whom the whole nation clusters, and all, ruler and people tied together by adamantine bands of patriotism."

These remarks of mine were based on observations of actual facts. In national unity Japan stands as an object lesson to the world; she furnishes an example which the world needs to copy, and which a nation so politically forlorn as ourselves more than any other needs to copy.

From the astounding success of Japan let us turn to the position the Great Republic of the United States of America occupies in the world, and take the lesson to heart of what Union can accomplish as we contrast their present position with the position that the handful of puritan pilgrims occupied when they first landed on American soil not quite three hundred years ago.

National Unity is our greatest need; it is the banner which we must raise up over our national life. National Unity must be engraven on the tablets of our minds and throb in the pulses of our hearts. There are mountains of difficulties before us, and if ever we must reach the goal we can only do so by being bound together like the bundle of faggots in the fable, with no weakening or loosening of the bands. Then perhaps we might once more be able to get an independent footing on the historical soil of our fathers, and perhaps once more rally round our own flag. A Japanese lives for the State, not for himself; we have no State for which to live, but let us live for our communities whilst we keep the hope in our hearts that communities grow into States.

We have grit and endurance in an unparalleled degree, but these characteristics will profit us nothing if we are wanting in unity.

Let us remember that utterance of the Founder of our faith. In our loyalty and allegiance to Him our life-blood has flowed like the torrents of a cataract, but we must remember His warning utterance:—

"What shall it profit a man." What shall it profit a nation. Unity is the soul of a nation. Let us keep our soul and not lose it.

THE ARMENIAN MASSACRES AND CIVILIZED EUROPE

"Hear then ye Senates! hear this truth sublime,
They who allow Oppression share the crime."

"A voice was heard in Ramah, lamentation, and bitter weeping; Rahel weeping for her children refused to be comforted for her children, because they were not."

In the twentieth century of the christian era, in the age of trumpeted progress, of boasted and vaunted civilization, there is a Ramah of countries, a desolated Ramah, blackened and calcined with the fires of oppression, and over her desolated wastes there flows, flows, continually flows, ever replenished and ever renewed, that red stream which crieth up from the earth to God: and out of this modern Ramah, a voice is heard of lamentation and bitter weeping, it riseth up in its boundless anguish to reach the heavens, it crieth out and will not be stopped, for it is the voice of the Rahel of nations weeping for her children and refusing to be comforted, because they are not.

Ah! thou Rahel of nations! to the cry of thy boundless anguish, to thy lamentation and bitter weeping, Christendom and Civilization, the Christendom and Civilization of Europe have replied "Are we thy children's keepers?"

Who that has read the history of the Crusades has not turned with sickening disgust from the chapters wherein history has recorded the savage barbarities and fearful excesses of those christian warriors, who went to Palestine ostensibly fired with the enthusiasm of a holy cause, but in reality only to glut in slaughter and gratify brutal passions. Europe has, however, designated her past as the "dark ages" into which she has thrust back, the ferocious outbursts of religion, the merciless persecutions of the church, the savage sweep of the barbarians of the north, and the unbridled tyrannies of despotic power, from all which she loudly boasts to have emancipated herself, and like the evolution according to the Darwinian theory of the anthropomorphal ape, to have progressed into the state of civilization. But beginning from the last quarter of the nineteenth and on into the first decade of the twentieth century, the horrors of the darkest ages in human history have lain at her doors, and towards these horrors Europe has kept up the role of an extenuatingly disclaiming, a mildly rebuking, sweetly frowning, smilingly denouncing, Disapprover.

Half a million Armenians annihilated by organized massacres of the most ferocious and hideous natures, and perhaps a corresponding number fated either to rot to death in Turkish prisons or made homeless and destitute to die of cold and starvation, with Europe nonchalantly looking on is surely convincing proof that the Humanity, Christianity and Civilization of Europe are whited sepulchres, hiding by the smooth outside the rottenness within; therefore ye priests of the gospel come down from your pulpits, close your churches, hold your tongues and be silent for ever, for the Christianity you preach has bowed itself out, if ever it existed, in Christian Europe. The Christ of Europe is the demon of greed and the demon of land hunger, and the god of civilization is Mammon.

In 1878 an astounding policy was carried out by Great Britain; it was the crowning act of her long continued support to Turkey, a government she knew to be hopelessly vicious and profoundly cruel and bad to the core. With this Power, England posing before the world as the home of freedom, the friend of the oppressed, and the defender of the rights and liberties of man, entered into a Convention. It was called the "Anglo-Turkish Convention," of which Article I reads thus:

"If Batum, Ardahan, Kars, or any of them, shall be retained by Russia, and if any attempt shall be made at any future time by Russia to take possession of any further territories of his Imperial Majesty the Sultan in Asia, as fixed by the definitive Treaty of Peace, England engages to join his Imperial Majesty the Sultan in defending them by force of arms. In return his Imperial Majesty the Sultan promises to England to introduce necessary reforms, to be agreed upon later between the two Powers, into the government and for the protection of the Christian and other subjects of the Porte in these territories. And in order to enable England to make necessary provision for executing her engagement, his Imperial Majesty the Sultan further consents to assign the island of Cyprus to be occupied and administered by England."

It is well to remark here what was blazoned to the world at the time that part of those *"necessary reforms"* *"in these territories"* include twenty-two large organized massacres of Armenians (besides smaller ones) dating from September 30th, 1895 to December 29th, 1895; and be it remembered that these were massacres of a hideousness and ferocity of nature even devils could not rival; besides also other organized massacres by the Turkish Government of the same nature (large and small) both before and after that period.

The British press, followed by a large section of the British public, raged against what they called the advance of Russia in the East, as they had already raged for half a century past. It is astonishing how one nation can swallow its own camels and strain at the other's gnats.

However, this Anglo-Turkish Convention and the Congress at Berlin was the crowning act of England's support and defense of a power whose rule had been characterized by mis-rule, massacre and oppression. Her prime minister returned from the Congress of Berlin loudly proclaiming "Peace with Honour." Of that "Honour" Time has been the test, and Time has revealed to the world that "Peace" in its true character.

Dating from the Congress of Berlin the supreme tragedy of Armenia begins; deliberately and without compunction England revived the dying tyranny of Turkey for the Armenians, deliberately and without compunction she took away from them (a people politically the most helpless and forlorn of all civilized nations) the only protection they had of a powerful neighbour willing and able to enforce its protection, and rivetted on their necks the yoke of the cruellest oppressor that the world had yet known. The history of the rule of the house of Osman up to the thirty-fourth Padishah was knowledge enough and experience enough for the British Government and the British people, and yet in the last quarter of the civilized nineteenth century, the great and enlightened Christian power of Great Britain proceeded to carry out and complete this gigantic political crime of fastening on the necks of a struggling Christian people, the last remnants of an ancient civilization, the merciless yoke of their oppressors. From that time onward history must mark the course of the supreme tragedy of Armenia.

The bold move taken by the Patriarch Nerses of sending delegates to the Congress of Berlin cost the renowned prelate his life, his firm refusal to recall his delegates aroused the last fury of Turkey's Padishah; the Patriarch was stealthily murdered and his genius and great personal influence lost to the cause of his people.

But a loss greater than the loss of their beloved leader befell the Armenians in the assassination of the Emperor Alexander II, whose untimely death plunged Russia back into the night of ignorance, bigotry and superstition, of the savagery and slavery, out of the darkness of which he was leading her; the best and noblest of Czars was succeeded by a son whose policy shaped itself directly contrary to that of his father's, and Russia from being the help of the Armenians under Turkish rule turned into one of the pillars of support of their oppressor.

"Since 1884," writes Mr. James Bryce, "it has been generally understood in Constantinople that the Russian Embassy has made no serious effort to bring about any radical change in Turkish administration, and it was indeed believed that the more England remonstrated the more did Russia point out to the Sultan how much he had erred in supposing that England was his friend."

We have it on the authority of Professor Arminius Vambéry that the Czar Alexander III had given assurances of his friendship and support to Sultan Abdul Hamid; and there are not wanting political students who affirm that the Armenian Massacres were in part instigated by Russian politicians who saw, or professed to see, in a free Armenia an impediment to Russia's advance in the south and a fostering of the spirit of independence in the Russian provinces of Armenia.[9] This on the authority of Mr.

---

[9] Nicholas C. Adossides [Youngest Son of Adossides Pasha] in the "Cosmopolitan" for July, 1909, ("Abdul the Dethroned") writes as follows:

"I remember the following incident which depicts the official Russian attitude: One night, while dining at the Russian legation in Bern, Switzerland, many Russian officials being present, the conversation was directed to the ever-engrossing Eastern question. A diplomat from St. Petersburg expressed his admiration of Abdul Hamid, praising his extraordinary intelligence and diplomatic skill. 'Besides,' he continued, 'he is not so black as his enemies have painted him.'

"Not being able to restrain my indignation at this, I protested, saying he was an arch assassin. 'Not to speak of his innumerable cruelties and many villainies,' I said, 'can you deny, Sir, that he instigated and accomplished the annihilation of 360,000 Armenians?'

"The admirer of the Sultan smiled, but before he could answer me, the military attaché of the legation, who was sitting next to me, exclaimed:

James Bryce was the reason which Prince Lobanoff assigned for his refusal to give support to British proposals of coercion towards Turkey. "On January 16, 1896," so writes Mr. Bryce, "when the massacres had gone on for more than three months, he (Prince Lobanoff) 'saw nothing to destroy his confidence in the bonne volonté of the Sultan, who was' ("he felt assured") 'doing his best.'" And Mr. Bryce continues to add "Turkey, which in 1877 had looked to England for help against Russia, now turned to Russia for support against the menaces of England."

We have it also on the authority of Mr. Bryce that shortly after the terrible and cold-blooded massacre of Armenians at Constantinople "the German Ambassador presented to the Sultan a picture of the German Imperial family which he had asked for some time ago"[10] and the friendship of Kaiser Wilhelm for Abdul Hamid "his friend and brother," as an American writer has called him; the costly gifts presented by the ex-Sultan to the German Imperial family, the magnificent reception of the Kaiser at Constantinople, and the still more magnificent concession of Turkish territory to Germany, are too well known to the world to need any further comment.

"If you condemn the Sultan for that, you astonish me. The Armenians? Bah! They ought to be exterminated en masse, and the Sultan did an excellent piece of work when he got rid of them. I have no use for them. Besides,' he continued, 'can't you see that a free Armenia would be a serious obstacle to Russian expansion and to our advance to the south and into Persia? Abdul Hamid has proved himself a very valuable ally of Russia. He is the best Ambassador at Constantinople that we've ever had." — Note to 2nd printing.

[10] This statement is corroborated by Dr. George Washburn in his account of the Constantinople Massacre: "But the Concert of Europe did nothing. It accepted the situation. The Emperor of Germany went further. He sent a special embassy to present to the Sultan a portrait of his family as a token of his esteem." — "Fifty Years in Constantinople," George Washburn. (Note to 2nd printing.)

Thus it became the fate of the unfortunate Armenians to be the bruised and mangled shuttle-cock of powerful bats.

NERSES VARJABETIAN

(Armenian Patriarch of Constantinople)

Much has been written and much has been said by great authorities, (far more comprehensively and by pens much more forcible than my humble efforts could aspire to reach) against the selfishness and callousness, the inhumanity and cynicism of those great powers which have coldly looked on and permitted the hellish atrocities and horrors of the Armenian Massacres. The name of William Ewart Gladstone is loved and revered by Armenians all over the world; but the thunderings of that veteran statesman and the denouncing protests of those thoughtful men whose feelings of revolted humanity have made themselves heard in sounding language, have fallen on stony ground; they have been like the voices of men crying out in the wilderness. Europe has turned a deaf ear to the condemnations of justice and truth, even as she has turned a deaf ear to the voice of Rahel weeping for her slaughtered children.

The victim of Abdul Hamid's revenge who was stealthily murdered in his bed. He was elected Patriarch in 1843 and held the highest place in the esteem and affection of his people. Mr. James Bryce gives his age at the time of his election in 1843 as seventy-three; if this is correct then he was over a hundred years old when he was foully murdered. Mr. Bryce writes of him as, "the worthy leader of his nation," "a man of high character and great ability."

A writer signing himself Beyzadé gives the following account of the Patriarch's tragic death in the July number of "The Wide World:"

> The attempted poisoning and subsequent death of Monseigneur Nercès Varjabétian, the Armenian Patriarch and Archbishop of Constantinople, was a revolting illustration of the inhuman and barbarous tactics of the Yildiz Kiosk "Camarilla." Monseigneur Nercès Varjabétian was not only one of the most prominent prelates of the Armenian Church, but was also a fearless patriot—a distinguished linguist, an eloquent preacher, and a thorough gentleman in every sense of the word. When peace was concluded between Turkey and Russia, and preparations were being made for the Berlin Congress, it was he who, in spite of the feared fanatical uprising of the Turks, threw prudence to the winds and took a step that will long be remembered in the annals of Armenian history.
>
> At the first meeting of the Berlin Congress the Turkish delegates were thunderstruck to learn from official sources that an Armenian delegation had arrived from Constantinople, sent by Monseigneur Nercès, the Patriarch, their object being to request the signatory Powers of the Berlin Treaty to force a guarantee from the Turkish Government to make certain important improvements in Armenia.

Abdul Hamid and his advisers were furious at this affront, and Monseigneur Nercès was summoned to the Palace. It is said that when he received the summons he simply smiled and asked one of his curates to read the Burial Service to him, as he did not expect to return alive. However, he went. No one has ever heard what passed between the Sultan and himself at the interview; suffice it to say that he immediately summoned the Armenian General Assembly and tendered his resignation. This was not accepted by the Assembly, and, amidst enthusiastic cheers, he was carried back to his apartments at the Patriarchate. Meanwhile a peremptory order reached him, signed by the Sultan, to recall the Armenian delegation from Berlin. This Monseigneur Varjabétian point-blank refused to do, and retired to his private residence at Haskeuy, a village on the Golden Horn. The success of the delegation, however, did not come up to his expectations. The Armenians, as it happened, could not be heard, but they were so far successful as to have an article inserted in the treaty.

The Sultan and his advisers never forgave the Patriarch this, though they could not openly do anything to him on account of his enormous popularity. Time passed on, and to all appearance the incident was forgotten, but it was not so. One summer afternoon a most cordial invitation was sent by a very high dignitary of the Palace, requesting the Archbishop to dine with him informally. An invitation of this kind could not very well be refused, so the Archbishop, accompanied only by a body-servant named Vartan, repaired to the Pasha's house. The Pasha received him at the door and escorted the visitor with much ceremony and extreme courtesy to a private apartment of the salamlik of his house (the men's quarters), where dinner was served. The geniality displayed by his host dispelled any fears that the Archbishop might have had as to his personal safety.

After dinner, as usual, coffee was served. Now, this serving of the coffee is rather a ceremonial according to high Turkish etiquette, and it is not unusual for guests to bring their own *tchooboukdar* (the servant who carries his master's pipe and pouch and also superintends the making of his coffee). The Archbishop was presented with a "tchoobouk" (pipe) filled and lighted for smoking, and a servant followed with coffee. The Archbishop accepted both with due compliments to his host, and took a sip at his coffee. Just at that moment the heavy curtains over the doorway were thrown apart, revealing the ghastly pale face of his servant Vartan, who cried, in Armenian, in a voice trembling with emotion, "Monseigneur, I did not brew the coffee!"

This was enough for the Archbishop; he pretended to be startled and spilt the coffee, but, alas! he had already drunk a small quantity of it. Meanwhile a scuffle was going on behind the *portière*, where his poor servant Vartan was paying the penalty of his devotion to his master. Concerning Vartan's whereabouts or his ultimate end nothing was ever made public—the poor fellow simply vanished. Monseigneur Varjabétian, after a short interval thanked the Pasha for his generous and kind hospitality and took his departure. On the way home he was taken violently ill and a doctor was hastily summoned. The Patriarch took to his bed, and lost all his hair through the effects of the poison. Then, one morning, when a servant took his breakfast upstairs he found, to his horror, that both the bedroom door and the window were wide open and his beloved master lay dead in his bed, which was covered with blood! There are no such things as coroners and juries in Turkey to ascertain the causes of mysterious deaths of this kind, but the news that the Patriarch was dead spread like wildfire through Constantinople. The Sultan himself thought it advisable to show some concern in the matter, and aides-de-camp from the Palace were sent to the Patriarchate to learn the full details of this "sad catastrophe," as they termed it. The official statement was that the Archbishop died of dysentery. Only a very few know how the Archbishop had died, and they wisely kept their mouths shut.

I was told the details of this story by a high official of the Armenian Patriarchate. It seems that as the poison did not act as quickly as the Patriarch's enemies had anticipated, owing to his having been cautioned in the nick of time, they "had to resort to other means"! The funeral was the largest ever witnessed in Constantinople, with an escort of Turkish cavalry sent specially by the Sultan, and representatives of all the religious denominations and the Diplomatic Corps. I was myself present, representing a foreign Government.

PART II

OUT OF THE DEPTHS

"Oh that my head were waters and mine eyes a fountain of tears, that I might weep day and night for the slain of my people."

A book has been written and published in Japan, its title "Niku Dan" translated into English, reads, "Human Bullets." This little book, a narrative of the siege of Port Arthur, after being read through the length and breadth of the empire, found translators to translate it into the best known of languages; and its young author, himself an actor in the siege, was summoned to the presence of his sovereign to be thanked and praised. The book is a graphic narrative of the most terrible siege in history, wherein is vividly portrayed the deadly struggle of the besiegers. It contains as an acknowledgement of its merit, a page on which is recorded the Field Marshal's appreciation, and another page bearing the Commanding General's commendation.

In simple narrative the author carries the reader through appalling scenes of horror, and as we read we are made to realize the slaughter of the enemy's machine guns, of their ground-mines, electric-wire entanglements, and exploding shells; we are made to hear the roar of the artillery fire dealing death and destruction, and there rises before us the mental vision of the fierce hand to hand conflict, and the dead and dying lying thickly in the dark ravine.

> "For hill and battle plain,
> With dying men and slain,
> Grew mountain heights of pain,
> And mine is boundless woe."

The grim warrior who stormed and took the most impregnable fortress in the world gives expression to his feelings on his own great achievement, in saddest words.

> "And mine is boundless woe,"

For the grim warrior's heart is cleft in twain for the human bullets that under his command hurled themselves to their death.

In the world's greatest war, human bullets were sacrificed for the protection of hearths and homes and a nation's existence, moreover the human bullets were made of men who fought and died for sovereign and country.

But there is a counter picture of horrors in which also there has been a sacrifice of human bullets, made not only of men but of women and children, human bullets, not of soldiers, themselves fortified and equipped with instruments of slaughter for fighting and grappling with the foe, but human bullets of unarmed men, of helpless women and children, of youth and old age, caught like rats in a rat-trap; and these human bullets have been sacrificed to the savage lusts of murder and plunder of the world's fiercest oppressors, and to the political and commercial interests of civilized nations.

In the first decade of the civilized twentieth century, a horrible and wanton slaughter of unarmed men, of helpless women and children has been perpetrated with all the accessories of cruelties unsurpassed for their fiendishness: whole towns and villages have been desolated, homes pillaged and destroyed, not only men, but women and children subjected to hideous deaths and nameless horrors, which no pen could depict in their true realism, and the details could never go into print, and this wanton slaughter, even as the many of a similar nature that have preceded it, has come and gone like a ripple on a smooth sea.

No cry of horror has risen from the hearts of civilized nations! Turkey can butcher the helpless victims of her greed and carnivorous instincts with impunity, since Christendom and Civilization are busy only with Turkish concessions, with land grabbing and money making.

"Human Bullets"! "Human Bullets"! here are human bullets of heavier rain than at the world's grimmest siege; here are "sure death detachments" hurled to a more pitiful fate; and the civilized world does not care, for Armenian Massacres come and go, and the civilized world is getting used to them. But in the eternal order of things, a Nemesis follows human actions, be they of individuals or of nations. Material Prosperity is a great and good thing, but Moral Prosperity is greater and better. The Armenians may be done to their death, the last remnants of an ancient civilization may be exterminated and consigned in their blood to oblivion; but to the nations grown great in material prosperity that for their own selfish interests can allow and condone this hellish extermination, history teaches a mighty lesson. The moral cancer eating into the moral sense of nations, saps moral prosperity which in its turn undermines material prosperity. Great Empires once flourishing have decayed through moral poverty. History repeats itself.

WHAT THE TURKISH CONSTITUTION MEANS FOR THE ARMENIANS

A year has passed since the inauguration of the Turkish Constitution; since the first glad cries of "liberty, fraternity, equality" were resounded as heralds of the peace and prosperity that were to follow; but although a whole year has passed, the Turkish Constitution, thus far, has only paraded itself as a spectacular effect, and as a panorama on shifting sand.

A whole year has passed and the liberal Turks have produced neither a Prince Ito nor an Abraham Lincoln, though both were urgently needed to meet the pressing exigencies and heavy responsibilities of the times; and we may well ask now, Where is the man who is to hold the helm of the Constitutional ship and steer it over the turbulent waters?

The task of the new régime was the most difficult that could have fallen to any administration. Beset on the one hand by the jealousies, rivalries, and political intrigues of European Powers; on the other, by the machinations of that "Red Beast" the ex-Sultan and his murderous and corrupt clique, by disappointed plundering pashas and officials (compelled to grant their arch enemy the ex-Sultan a lease of life through fear of a fanatical populace), the liberal Turks on their own part have not brought to bear upon their work any administrative ability, when extraordinary powers of governing and the highest and strongest genius for administration were absolutely needed. The Turk has always shown to the world that he is a born fighter, but a puerile administrator.

For the Armenians the Constitution has resulted in two conditions—Massacre and Oppression; their hopes and aspirations have ended in the death throes of, as some accounts give, thirty thousand and others fifty thousand of their unhappy race, in homelessness and precipitation into absolute destitution of a few more thousands,[11] and in insecurity for the nation at large. An unarmed population scattered and dispersed among a hostile, murderous and fanatical populace; their position even under the new régime is to be compared to that of herbivorous animals standing at bay in the midst of ravening wolves.

His spiritual interests call upon the Moslem Turk and the Moslem Kurd to murder the Christian Armenian; his material interests to plunder and enrich his own idleness with the worldly goods the other has acquired by his industry and toil, and the prosperity and well-being that the Armenian labours to bring to the fairest provinces under the sun are swooped upon and devastated by the brigandage of his enemies. Religious fanaticism and lust of plunder have always been governing elements in the Turkish massacres, and against these same religious fanaticism and lust of plunder, the Armenians stand to-day in deadly peril under the new régime.

What more is to follow? Our hearts sicken to forecast, and our minds tremble to foresee. Are the balance of our striplings and our greybeards, our pen-men, and our ploughmen to be made to rot in Turkish dungeons, condemned to such loathsome horrors as can only be perpetrated in Turkish prisons? Are the balance of our women to be subjected to agonies so hideous and revolting that death at the fiery stake or on the iron rack were mercy and bliss? Are the balance of our babes and children to be exterminated like vermin? Are the balance of our people, the industrious, intelligent, clean, self-respecting element in the Turkish Empire, to be yet again hunted like wild beasts and killed like rats and flies?

---

[11] Since these lines were written later accounts show that over a hundred thousand have been precipitated into homelessness and destitution, and this misery is growing greater every day.—Note to 2nd printing.

We are not wild and lawless descendants of Jenghis Khan and Tamerlane: we are peace-loving, law-abiding citizens, lovers of language and literature, of the arts and sciences, energetic traders, hardworking tillers of the soil, industrious artizans and labourers, producing in ourselves all the elements that constitute the society and well-being of civilized man; and as the oldest Christians, we ask of Christian nations, if we are to be trodden out?

On the soil of our fatherland we are surrounded by a murderous, marauding, religion-frenzied populace, and neither Humanity nor Christianity will hold out to us a helping hand.

If nothing else were done for the Armenians, at least Christian governors should be appointed over the provinces inhabited by them: we do not expect the Turkish Government to do this of their own initiative, but we have a right to expect the European Powers that were signatories to the Treaty of Berlin to compel the new régime to do it. Since the signing of the famous Treaty of Berlin thirty-one years ago, the history of the Armenians has been written in blood and tears, as the history of no other nation has been written before or now; and we ask, How long? How long will the Christian Powers stand silent witnesses to the work of slaughter and oppression carried on under their eyes?

Alas! the weight of the Turkish bonds is too heavy in the scale, and Armenian life too light; the selfish interests of the European Powers involved in the Turkish Empire cannot be endangered to save the blood of three or four millions of Armenians, and the death warrant of an oppressed and bleeding nation can find no place on the table of the Hague Conference of Peace and Civilization.

THE ARMENIAN QUESTION

In the closing pages of "Twenty Years of the Armenian Question" published in 1896, its distinguished author,[12] one of the greatest authorities on the subject, makes the following notable comment on the character and fate of the Armenian race.

"They had maintained their nationality from immemorial times, before history began to be written. They had clung to their Christian faith, under incessant persecution for fifteen centuries. They were an intelligent, laborious race, full of energy, and increasing in numbers wherever oppression and murder did not check their increase, because they were more apt to learn, more thrifty in their habits, and far less infected by Eastern vices than their Mahommedan neighbours. They were the one indigenous population in Western Asia which, much as adversity had injured them, showed a capacity for moral as well as intellectual progress, and for assimilating the civilization of the West. In their hands the industrial future of Western Asia lay, whatever government might be established there; and those who had marked the tenacity and robust qualities of the race looked to them to restore prosperity to these once populous and flourishing countries when the blighting shadow of Turkish rule had passed away. But now, after eighteen years of constantly increasing misery, a large part, and, in many districts, the best part, of this race has been destroyed, and the remnant is threatened with extinction."

These remarks made in 1896 by a great and disinterested authority with a profound knowledge of the subject he was writing about, stand as true to-day as when they were written.

---

[12] "Transcaucasia and Ararat: Twenty Years of the Armenian Question," James Bryce.—Note to 2nd printing.

From 1896 onwards, events following in succession one upon another have proved the truth and soundness of his opinions.

Can the Armenians hope now for any change in their condition under Turkish rule? To this question, we must answer an emphatic No!

The causes that must operate against any change are many and deep-seated. In the first place it cannot be expected that a few Turks of liberal ideas (or it may be French polished) at Constantinople, are going to change the thought and character of the nation. The characteristics of a people change very slowly, if they ever change at all, and the predominant national traits of the many-blooded modern Turk have been shown to the world to be, cruelty and fanaticism, combined with a fierce sensuality; and what is more than all, and which has to be remembered most, is, that they are a people accustomed to the unbridled gratification of their worst passions.

The ethnographic traits of the Turkman which history bears out, are wildness and fierceness, and it would not be incorrect to argue that with the instincts of his primitive ancestors have been assimilated the many cross currents that run in his veins, into all of which has been infused the doctrines of the religion of the sword, a religion which does not make for the peace or well being of mankind; a religion, also, which assigning one of the two sexes to the degraded position of being created solely for the gross pleasure of the other, does not make for the exaltation of mankind.

To quote again the eminent authority previously referred to: "No Mahommedan race or dynasty has ever shown itself able to govern well even subjects of its own religion, while to extend equal rights to subjects of a different creed is forbidden by the very law of its being."

Not the Jewish conceit proclaiming itself God's elect and chosen, and originating the name "heathen" which it scorned. Not the Christian conceit emanating from the Jewish source, and laying the flattering unction to its soul of superiority over the "heathen" of its own time. Not the unbending caste exclusiveness of the Brahman across whose path even the shadow of the despised Sudra falling would be deemed defilement. Not any of these, can equal the intolerant religious pride of the Mahommedan, or reach the pinnacle of religious self-sufficiency on which he has seated himself. To be a Mahommedan, is enough—*Cela suffit*.

To any one who has familiar acquaintance with Mahommedans, and intimate with Mahommedan thought, one fact must strike itself most forcibly, and that is, the Mahommedan is above all things a Mahommedan. His religion is the paramount question in his life, and remains its predominating feature above everything else. This should not be surprising, since to the "faithful" Paradise is secured, and all crimes and transgressions against "unbelievers" absolved.

Added to these important factors of racial characteristics, influences of religion, and long grown habits of the Turk, we have also in Turkish Armenia another evil, from which the other provinces of the Turkish Empire fortunately for themselves have been exempt; this super-added evil, is, the large neighbouring bodies of Kurds and Circassians, greater marauders and depredators than the Turks, the regular occupation of whose lives comprises murder and robbery, and who have through weary centuries unremittingly quartered themselves upon the industrious christian peasants, and lived on the fruits of their labour and toil. Indeed as the Hamidieh cavalry which was established expressly for the Hamidian massacres was composed of these Kurds, it ought to be matter of speculation what outlet these warriors, trained and practised in organized murder, can now find for those habits in which they were encouraged and trained to indulge by the Hamidian régime.

Under all such conditions no hope of better days can be forthcoming, no prospect of better times seems possible, for that unhappy portion of the Armenian race whom force of circumstances keeps on the soil of the fatherland.

The appointment of Christian governors over the provinces inhabited by them might ameliorate some of the evils, or the other alternative, of allowing the use of arms to all alike, irrespective of creed or nationality, would furnish some means of self-defence against the raids and barbarities of the oppressors; but even if such concessions were granted, life for the christian peasant subject to Turkish rule, and living in the midst of his enemies, must remain one long struggle and battle against pillage, murder, depredation, and offences of the worst nature. Not the most fertile soil, not the most favourable climatic conditions, not the most assiduous industry, not the most peace loving, law abiding instincts, can bring to the Armenian peasant under Turkish rule even a modicum of that comfort, happiness, and security of life and property, which the law of all civilized countries guarantees to the industrious labourer and tiller of the soil.

OPEN LETTER TO THE HONORABLE PRESIDENT WILLIAM HOWARD TAFT

Excellent Sir,

You are the President of the mighty Republic of the United States of America, and I am only an obscure unit of a forlorn and helpless nation, but encouraged by the intrinsic qualities of your head and heart, and also by the record of great and noble services rendered in the cause of oppressed humanity, by certain of your predecessors in the presidential chair (so encouraged) I venture humbly to address you. The annals of that presidential chair on which you sit are clear and bright as the noonday sun; turning over the pages of their brightness, I am encouraged to address you its present occupant.

Your immediate predecessor rendered a great service in the interests of Humanity, by bringing a terrible and bloody war to its close. His staunch strong hand of friendship was held out to the gallant nation fighting heroically for its national existence, whilst the might of his iron will strenuously contested and made the peace which will ever be associated with his name, but there was a peace which his great heart wished to break but could not succeed in breaking, and which his upright mind has branded as "infamous": such are his own words "the infamous peace kept by the joint action of the great powers, while Turkey inflicted the last horrors of butchery, torture and outrage upon the men, women and children of despairing Armenia."[13] For thirty-one years the great European Powers kept up by joint action an infamous peace, and out of regard for their own selfish interests allowed a corrupt, vicious, gangrened and blood-thirsty power

---

[13] "The Strenuous Life: Expansion and Peace," Theodore Roosevelt.—Note to 2nd printing.

to wreak its hellish atrocities not only on the men, but on the women and children of a helpless nation.

These are strong words, but they are true, and you will agree with me that the meanest and humblest of God's creatures has a right to speak the truth, and that greatest is the right to speak the truth, when it is spoken in the cause of murdered, outraged and misery-stricken humanity.

The yoke of Turkey rivetted on the necks of the Armenians by England in 1878, was rivetted again by Russia, and yet again rivetted by Germany. The political interests and the commercial interests of Europe have trampled us under foot; we have been sacrificed on the altar of the political animosities of England and Russia, and given over, men, women and children to butchery, slaughter, imprisonment, torture; we have been crushed under the iron wheels of the Baghdad railway, a greater Juggernauth for us, while the ex-Sultan received his payment and "bartered a kingdom for the Kaiser's friendship"; and yet again we have been crushed when British diplomacy checkmated William of Hohenzollern's dream.

The death warrant of our bleeding nation has found no place on the table of the Hague Conference of Peace and Civilization since the selfish interests of the European Powers would give it no abiding room. President of a great and free Republic, let it be the work of your mighty hands to lay it there. The Cabinets of Europe have turned a deaf ear to the death shriek of our bleeding nation, let our despairing cry be heard now in the Senate of the United States of America.

It remains for the historian of the future to record the Armenian Massacres as the foulest blot and the blackest stain on European Civilization and European International Morality, but in addressing you now I will turn down the pages of the hideous Past, and humbly lay open the pages of the Present, on which is clearly written the deadly peril in which our nation stands: the book is open, and who will may read. For it is not the goodwill of the new régime that has to be taken into calculation, as far as the Armenians are concerned, but the powerfulness or the powerlessness of the new régime to make for their protection.

How can we forget Adana? A whole town and villages sacked and desolated; fifty thousand of our men, women and children done to horrible deaths, and the residue left to homelessness and starvation. How can we forget that the arch-enemy of Christian and liberal Turk still lives, dethroned but not executed, and that through fear of his worshippers and his adherents the liberal Turks are compelled to pamper and support the monster assassin of the world? When such difficulties beset the path of the liberal Turks, the rulers, what security is there for a subject people, alien in race and religion?

President of a great and free Republic, we need a friend, we ask for your mighty hands to be held out to us in succour, since the number of our enemies are legion: even Nature has arrayed herself against us in the inexorable conditions of the physical geography of our country. Shall the President of a mighty Republic with noble traditions; shall the christian men and women of the United States leave us to our terrible fate?

"To serve Armenia is to serve Civilization." These words were spoken by a great and revered statesman; the noble handiwork of his Creator (William Ewart Gladstone), now gone to his honored rest. "Do not let me be told that one nation has no authority over another" was his reply to the Armenian deputation which waited on him in 1894. Let his reply be your answer to us now, President of a mighty Republic; let it be your answer written in golden letters across the banner of that great civilization, of which you are the presiding head.

The Republic of the United States of America has been compared to that grain of mustard seed, which when planted in the earth budded forth and grew into such dimensions that the birds of the air lodged under the branches thereof. I pray that the shadow of those branches be extended over my bleeding nation.

ABDUL HAMID, THE TRIUMPH OF CRIME

A monster assassin! Has he been brought before the bar of his country, tried and condemned to the penalty of death, such as in the days of his power he meted out to hundreds of thousands of innocents? Has he been cast into a loathsome prison, such as the many in which thousands of his victims have rotted and died? Nay! not so! it is not so decreed in Turkey.

In Turkey, a camarilla of murderous and plundering pashas, and a fanatical and marauding populace stand behind a Padishah who knew how to furnish gratification for the murdering and marauding instincts of his adherents. Nay! neither death nor imprisonment for the Padishah whose sovereignty was the most auspicious for brigandage and murder. Who dares to slay or imprison the demigod of rapine and despotism? Such things cannot be done in Turkey.

For crimes that were in comparison as light as air, those puerile tyrants, Charles of England and Louis of France forfeited their heads. Poor Charles and Louis! Your heads chopped off and your bodies trundled away in a cart: no glorifying spiritualized titles of Zeid and Imam read out in your bills of indictment; such glorifying spiritualized titles are reserved for monster assassins in Turkey.

In Turkey, a monster assassin whose list of murders rank him as premier assassin of the world, who under heel of iron and fire annihilated the rights and liberties of his subjects is pensioned off to live in purple and fare sumptuously: housed in a luxurious palace, he sits on carpeted divans, supported by silken and velvet pillows, with eleven ministering houris, the youngest and fairest of his past entourage, to solace the "dolce far niente" of his deposed Padishahdom. Ample leisure, possible opportunities to hatch plots for the subversion of law and order, and the revival of the reign of plunder and massacre. But it is so allowed in Turkey. It is enough to be a Caliph and a Padishah to be able to count victims, not by thousands, but by hundreds of thousands, and remain immune from punishment for mountains of crime.

What evil, what woe and desolation hast thou not wrought, spiritualized Zeid and Imam, Caliph and Padishah? And yet thou art allowed to live! Evil genius of thy people! thou hast worked out their moral degradation to the lowest depths that a nation could fall; but limitless evil, supremest woe, hast thou worked over the nation whose country thou turned into a charnel house of slaughter, and over whom thy reign of thirty-three years hung like a pestilence. Who can count the multitude of thy crimes against them, who can measure the height and the depth of the woe that thou laid over their lives. Hearths and homes pillaged and desolated, harvest fields turned into rivers of blood, not thousands upon thousands, but hundreds of thousands of men, women, and children tortured with devilish ingenuities of torture, imprisoned in loathsome dungeons, outraged, butchered, slaughtered, hunted like wild beasts, left to homelessness and starvation.

Enough blood to drown a leprous souled and gangrened souled Padishah and his gangrened pack of followers! Enough crime to hang a Caliph!

Out with thy Caliphate! even by the law of thy prophet, that fierce son of the desert, the Caliph is ordained protector of the weak and helpless; what didst thou with thy thirty-three years of Caliphal power, except crush the weak and annihilate the helpless.

The very earth has echoed with the dying cry of the least of them, those "christian puppies" with little bodies piled up one upon another, and little heads struck off together at one stroke; with the frenzied shrieks of mothers who have seen with their own eyes the slaughter of their children, with the anguished wail of women, with the death groans of youth and old age. Aye! the very earth has echoed with the dying gasp of that righteous man, the venerable sire of his people, the renowned nonagenarian whom thou stealthily silenced on a bloody bed into the sleep of death for trying to save his flock from thy hyena jaws.

An explosive bomb shattered the life of thy crowned opponent, (a noble life consecrated to the welfare of his people) but no chance or opportunity directed any explosive bomb to shatter thy cadaverous body. No jeweled pistol or secret dagger like the many that have dripped with the blood of thy victims in thy Yildiz Kiosk, found its way to thy treacherous heart. No poisoned cup of coffee like the countless cups brewed in thy palaces trickled down thy throat to end thy vampire existence.

Thou hast lived! Protected from the Nemesis of thy crimes by the jealousies and rivalries of great powers which thou artfully played one against another; by the combined forces of religion and plunder which thou cunningly wielded into one. Even so thou livest! Peerless living example in the civilized twentieth century of the Triumph of Crime.

L'AVENIR

In the foregoing pages I have directed my humble efforts to sketch out what the Powers of Europe have done in the past, and how their actions have reflected on my unfortunate race.

It is considered good policy now by a certain class of European writers to ascribe all the horrors of the Armenian Massacres to Hamid the despot, to represent him as a tyrant as unassailable and unconquerable as he was implacable, in short as a sort of superhuman being who swept everything before him to the consummation of his own despotic will. The reason for this is not difficult to perceive. They would fain disavow the part Europe has played in the tragedy, and to do this successfully it becomes necessary also to present Turkey to the world now as a paradise (from whence the tyrant once removed) peopled only by saints and angels; so we have also many roseate colored word pictures of Constitutional Turkey.

The murders, deportations and imprisonments of the Turkish revolutionaries, or more correctly reformers, were undoubtedly the sole work of Abdul Hamid and his palace clique, but Abdul and his minions could not have carried out that hellish work of wholesale extermination of the Armenians without the perpetration and participation of the Turkish people. It is true the massacres were originated and organized in the Palace, the Palace clique stirred up religious fanaticism and race hatred, but the co-operation of the people was necessary; and the people co-operated in order to plunder and enrich themselves with the worldly goods that the Armenians always knew how to acquire by their own industry and toil; the appeal to their marauding and bestial instincts met with a ready response. It was moreover easy work for a race of brigands, especially as their numbers exceeded their victims by about ten to one and who were practically unarmed.

The first Armenian Massacres of Abdul Hamid were tentative; he began by feeling the pulse of Europe; he found that the six Signatories to the Treaty of Berlin accepted the situation, he was thus emboldened to carry out that long and awful list of horrors that stands without its parallel in history. Clearly it was in the power of Europe to have prevented both the massacres and all the agonizing sufferings that came in their train, but Europe took no preventive action.

Let us ask the question, Who and what are these Turks, whom Europe for her own sordid ends has petted and pampered and helped and supported? and the answer comes with striking force to-day over the lapse of a century, in the words of one of England's greatest sons: "I have never before heard that the Turkish Empire has been considered any part of the balance of Powers in Europe. They despise and contemn all Christian princes as infidels, and only wish to subdue and exterminate them and their people. What have these worse than savages to do with the Powers of Europe but to spread war, destruction, and pestilence among them? The Ministers and the policy which shall give these people any weight in Europe will deserve all the bans and curses of posterity."[14]

To-day the Powers of Europe are armed to the teeth. To-day they are groaning under the burden of armaments which they are increasing with breathless speed although the burden grows heavier. To-day all Europe is trembling lest the hell-hounds of war be let loose. Has any political student put his finger on the cause which began, the beginning and the source of the evil, the Alpha of the Omega. I have put my finger on it—the beginning and the source—The jealousies and rivalries of European Politics in the Turkish Empire. According to an Eastern proverb "The

---

[14] Edmund Burke—Speech in Parliament in opposition to Mr. Pitt, 1791.—Note to 2nd printing.

flies are always round the honey," but sometimes the flies stick in the honey.

Politicians of the Governments of Europe have said in the pride of their hearts "There is no God." Particularly has this spirit of cynicism and heartlessness governed the actions of Russian politicians after the death of Alexander II. Since 1881, they have looked upon the extermination of the Armenians just as the pathfinder in a forest would look upon a dense forest growth, the clearing away of which would make out a path for him and lead to running streams and harvest fields. In the eyes of Russian politicians the unfortunate Armenians have been the forest growth which has stood in the way of their advance to the South and into Persia, and they have looked on with intense satisfaction at the exterminating process of the Turk, which they have regarded as the helping hand that clears away the difficulty confronting them. But precisely whether Russia can grow strong by the pouring out of Armenian blood, and whether her empire will be extended by their hellish extermination remains to be solved by the future. One thing, however, the history of the world points out, that iniquity ends, not in strength, but in dissolution; and "The wages of sin is death."

Politicians of Europe have, in the pride of their hearts, arrogated to themselves that power, which appertains to the Creator; they have imagined that they hold the world in the hollows of their hands, and the misery or happiness of millions of human beings has weighed as nothing in their estimation, against the interests of what they have designated "our sphere of influence," but they have forgotten what they need to be reminded that the Creator is mightier than the creature and that the eternal law of heaven and earth changeth not for politicians.

"And the First Morning of Creation wrote;
What the Last Dawn of Reckoning shall read."

"Of old hast thou laid the foundation of the earth; and the heavens are the work of thy hands.

"They shall perish, but thou shalt endure: yea, all of them shall wax old like a garment; as a vesture shalt thou change them, and they shall be changed. But thou art the same, and thy years shall have no end."

When the heavens and earth shall perish, shall wax old as a garment and be changed as a vesture; whence shall endure the power and principalities, the empires and spheres of influence of him who is called man?

"As for man, his days are as grass; as a flower of the field, so he flourisheth. For the wind passeth over it, and it is gone; and the place thereof shall know it no more."

THE ORIGIN OF THE ARMENIANS—THE INTRODUCTION OF CHRISTIANITY INTO ARMENIA—DECLINE & GRAND REVIVAL

"God shall enlarge Japhet and he shall dwell in the tents of Shem, and Canaan shall be his servant."

For the interpretation of this blessing of Noah's to his eldest son, and of how it may or may not have met with its fulfilment, I shall leave to theologians to discuss, and only record it here as a quotation from Genesis. Beyond the story of his connection with the flood, and this blessing with which his father blessed him, and the genealogy of his sons, we read nothing more in Genesis, of Japhet, this mighty father of the Caucasian race.

The genealogy in Genesis runs thus:

"The sons of Japhet, Gomer and Magog and Madai, and Javan, and Tubal, and Meschech, and Tiras.

"And the sons of Gomer: Ashkenaz and Riphath and Togarmah.

"And the sons of Javan; Elishah and Tarshish, Kittim and Dodamin.

"By these were the isles of the Gentiles divided in their lands; every one after his tongue, after their families, in their nations."

Only the names of the three sons of Gomer, and the four sons of Javan are given in Genesis, and by these we are told were the isles of the Gentiles divided. So much for Genesis.

Later history records that these Gentiles spread themselves over part of that stretch of terra firma which now goes by the name of Europe, developing their own families, and their own nations, and originating their own tongues, and also they spread themselves over other parts of the surface of the globe, populating where they could, ruling where they could.

But through the roll of centuries which lost themselves into the flight of thousand years, one branch of the sons of Japhet kept themselves on the land where Noah planted his vineyard, and round the base of that mountain from whence his descendants began to spread and people the earth.

Tradition has woven a romance round the names of towns and villages in Armenia. "No aighee" (Noah's vineyard) is the name of a village supposed to be the place where the patriarch planted his vine; and "Nakhitchvan"[15] meaning (first descent) where Noah is supposed to have descended from the ark; also "Mairand" meaning (mother is there) where Noah's wife is supposed to be buried; and "Erivan"[16] meaning (that which can be seen) supposed to be the land in the distance which could be seen when Noah descended from the ark.

---

[15] Nakhitchvan—Invaded and seized by the Persian Monarch Shah Abbas in 1603. Taken from Persia by Russia in 1827.

[16] Erivan—Invaded and seized by the Persian monarch Shah Abbas in 1603. Taken from Persia by Russia 1827.

MINARET AT ERIVAN, ONE OF THE CITIES TRADITION ASCRIBES TO BE FOUNDED BY NOAH

Armenian history begins with Haik, the first chief or king of the tribe: he was third in descent from Japhet, and fourth in descent from Noah, and his genealogy is given thus: Haik the son of Togarmah, the son of Gomer, the son of Japhet, the son of Noah.

"They of the house of Togarmah traded in thy fairs with horses and horsemen and mules" is the designation given by Ezekiel, 27th chapter 14th verse of the merchants of Armenia trading with Tyrus.

Haik revolting from Belus, the Nimrod of Genesis, the son of Cush and grandson of Ham, retraced his footsteps from the plains of Shinar, where he with others had tried to build the tower whose top should reach into heaven, and with his followers and children settled himself round the base of Ararat.

Perhaps a nascent fire of patriotism was burning in Haik's heart as he retraced his steps to the land of his father's or grandfather's childhood: perhaps owing to the circumstances under which he was placed, he had not the alternative of another choice.

We read in Armenian history that Belus sent the following message to Haik:

"Why didst thou go to that cold country? Were it not better for thee to have moderated thy pride, and submissively dwelt on my territory in any part thou wished."

To which Haik replied:

"It is better to die bravely than to bow down in fear to that presumptuous man who would be worshipped as a god."

Whatever causes may have influenced Haik, his choice of country was geographically most unfortunate for the race he founded, and it may truly be said that owing to its geographical conditions affording facilities for the march of conquerors, to have been instrumental in bringing about the overwhelming and unequalled adversities that through weary centuries have followed like a grim fate the footsteps of his descendants.

No geographical position on the surface of the globe could have been more unfortunate, hemmed round by larger territories, with no natural defences or boundaries, and no outlet to the sea, except the lake of the Caspian on the one side, and the lake of the Black Sea on the other, that land on which Haik chose to found a country and a nation, has been soaked with the blood and the tears of this branch of the sons of Japhet.

The animosity between Haik and Belus continued, and later, according to Armenian historians, Belus was slain in battle by an arrow from the bow of Haik.

We read the following record of Belus in Genesis: "he began to be a mighty one in the earth." "He was a mighty hunter before the Lord: wherefore it is said, Even as Nimrod the mighty hunter before the Lord."

In Armenian history, Haik is depicted as a man of powerful physique and gigantic stature; no man of his time being able to bend his bow or shoot his arrow. Moses of Chorene, the chief of Armenian historians, quoting from the learned Syrian Mar Abbas, writes of him thus:

"He was graceful and well built, curly haired, pleasing in appearance, and strong armed, and it might be remembered that among the heroes of his time he was the most remarkable of all."

However that may be, Armenian history awards to Haik the proud distinction of having overcome and slain Belus, the mighty hunter Nimrod.

The people who retraced their steps from the plains of Shinar, and settled round the base of Ararat called themselves "Hai" after their chief, and they named their country "Haiyastan," and these names still continue to be used in the Armenian, or "Haiyérane" as the Armenians call their own language.

GREAT AND LITTLE ARARAT

I will pass over the periods when the son and grandson of Haik ruled over Armenia, and only mention that the mountain known to the world as Ararat was called by the Hai "Masis" after their king Amasia and great-grandson of Haik. To this day, Armenian peasants and others dwelling round Ararat, call the mountain "Masis." I remember in my childhood having seen an Armenian periodical entitled "Masis," which showed that the name had been steadily kept up.

I will again pass over the periods ruled by the successors of Amasia, and relate the story of King Aram, who ended his brilliant reign in B.C. 1796 after ruling over Armenia fifty-eight years.

He was a great and powerful prince, and extended his dominions, and grew to be so mighty in battle that the neighbouring nations called his country Aramia and the people were called Aramians, such names as Armenia or Armenians being no doubt later corruptions.

The first victory of Aram was over Neuchar king of Media, whom he took prisoner and put to death, and made a large part of the country of the defeated prince tributary to his own. The second victory of Aram was over Barsham king of Babylon, whom also he took prisoner and put to death. The next victory was over the king of Cappadocia; the army of the Cappadocians was pursued to the very shores of the Mediterranean, and the whole of Cappadocia fell into the hands of Aram B.C. 1796. Also Ninus king of Assyria, at one time an eager enemy, awed by the victories of Aram, sought to cultivate his friendship.

No doubt if the volumes and scripts of paper or parchment of the famous Alexandrian library, which burned for six months as fuel in the four thousand baths of the city, had escaped that most atrocious act of vandalism, and been preserved instead, vast treasures of knowledge now lost to us concerning the ancient kingdoms of Western Asia might be known in our day; and also when the tide of Islam victory rolled over the kingdom of Armenia, how much of the story and history of the people was lost and destroyed along with the destruction of their independence it would be difficult now to calculate or assert, but in taking up link by link of whatever knowledge has been left to us, there seems to be grounds for supposing that the "Aramæans" designated by foreign writers as "a people of Semitic race, language and religion, coming from Northern Arabia and settling in the region between the western boundaries of Babylonia and the highlands of Western Asia" were no other than the Hai who under their King Aram had spread their conquests and their kingdom into Mesopotamia and even to the shores of the Mediterranean.

Herodotus also rather corroborates this conjecture when he includes Northern Mesopotamia, together with the mountainous country of Ararat, under the name of Armenia, and in writing of the Armenian boats that brought merchandise to Babylon, he remarks that they were constructed in Armenia, *in the parts above Assyria.*

Archæological researches have laid the claim that the modern Armenians are the descendants of the old Hittites; the modern Armenian being supposed to be the survival of the ancient Hittite tongue, and it is asserted almost everything that is known in the Hittite language is Old Armenian in form: but who these Hittites were, or whence they came neither historian nor archæologist have been able definitely to ascertain. In the Armenian version of the Bible, we find the name "Kethosi" used for the Hittite who were known to the Assyrians and Egyptians as "Ketha," but this can have no important bearing since the Bible was translated into the Armenian language from the Greek in the fifth century of the Christian era, and the Armenian scribe no doubt simply translated what he found in the Greek.

According, however, to all known history the Hittites were a warlike and conquering race and ranked among the foremost of the nations of Western Asia. The modern historian has come to the following conclusion concerning them: "Their primitive home is thought to have been in that part of Armenia where the Euphrates, the Halys, and Lycus approach nearest to one another; and it is even asserted that the modern Armenians are descendants of the old Hittites. From this point they began their career of conquests, probably under the leadership of some able and vigorous chief, whose ambition overleaped his native boundaries. One conquest led to another. Their leaders acquired great armies, and subdued many nations, until the Hittites became one of the most powerful peoples of ancient times, and their kings were able successfully to defy even Egypt, at that time the strongest nation on the globe."

This description accords with Armenian history; the Hai being known from time immemorial as a warlike race, and extending their territory by conquests, until, as I have narrated, under the leadership of Aram their kingdom spread from the mountains of Upper Armenia to the shores of the Mediterranean and into northern Mesopotamia, which proves that almost all of Asia Minor was conquered by them, and according also to Armenian history the language of the Hai was introduced into Cappadocia by King Aram.[17]

Allowing, however, for the many obscurities of Armenian history, confusion comes in, when historians or archæologists ascribe a Mongolian ancestry to the Hittites, whereas Armenian history holds its unquestionable ground firmly and decidedly on the Japhetian ancestry; and the peculiar physiognomy of the Armenians; the oval contour of face, the distinctive, prominent nose, large eye, and well marked arch of eyebrow do not show any traces of Mongolian ancestry. It follows therefore that if the Armenians are the descendants of the Hittites, then the Hittites were not of Mongolian ancestry. If the Hittites were the Hai, the name must have undergone corruption during the course of centuries and it is reasonable to suppose that they shared the fate of all conquerors, and after a period of power, were driven back from the shores of the Mediterranean to their own native home.

Aram was succeeded by his son Ara, a prince of such singular and surpassing beauty that he was surnamed "Ara the Beautiful." The famous Semiramis, wife of Ninus king of Assyria, attracted by his great personal beauty offered him her affections and her throne after the death of her husband, but her proffers of love were scornfully rejected by Ara, who according to the story related of his own love was passionately attached to his queen Nuvard. The proud Semiramis, scorned, enraged and mortified, declared war against Ara and entered his country with her armies; a battle was fought in which Ara leading his army was slain, although Semiramis had given special

---

[17] The Hittites flourished in the sixteenth and fifteenth centuries B.C. King Aram completed his conquest of Cappadocia in B.C. 1796.

instructions to her troops to be careful of his life and bring him to her a living prisoner.

The death of Ara was evidently a grief to Semiramis, for she established his son Kardos on his father's throne. She also built a town and fortress on the shores of Lake Aghthamar, now called Van, the battlefield on which the beautiful Ara pursued by her fatal love lost his life. The town and fortress were named "Semiramakert" meaning "built by Semiramis."

The name of the highest mountain in Armenia which the people of the country called "Masis" came to be known as Ararat, it is supposed to be derived from the Armenian words "Ara-i-jard" meaning "the defeat of Ara" or "the undoing of Ara." If this version is correct, the name is likely to have been used in derision by the Assyrians. According to another version the name of Ara was converted into Ararat, and the country called after him. Thus we read in the account of the flood given in Genesis:

"And the ark rested in the seventh month, on the seventeenth day of the month, upon the mountains of Ararat."

In the Armenian version of the bible, we read "on the twenty-seventh day of the month," but likewise as in English "upon the mountains of Ararat." This is not surprising since the designation "thaghavoroothune Araratian" meaning "the kingdom of Ararat" is in use in the Armenian language.

I have alluded to the reigns of Aram and Ara to show how the Hai have come to be called Armenians and how their country has come to be named Armenia; also whence the name, Ararat; and as I purport here only to treat of the origin of the Armenians, I shall now pass on to the no less interesting period of their history: THE INTRODUCTION OF CHRISTIANITY.

When that great event bearing the message "on earth peace,

goodwill toward men" celebrated throughout the Christian world as the divine birth, took place in the city of Bethlehem; Abgar the son of Arsham reigned in Armenia.

That country was now broken in strength, the severe blows dealt on the one side by the Roman Empire, and the incessant warfare of the Persian on the other, had greatly curtailed her former independence and power; the talons of the Roman Eagles were already felt in her vitals, and the king of Armenia subsisted under the favor of the Roman Emperor, whilst it became necessary for him to cultivate the friendship of his powerful neighbour, the king of Persia.

Whilst in Persian territory, whither he had gone to settle the dispute that had arisen on the death of the Persian monarch between his sons, Abgar had contracted a severe disease, evidently leprosy.

ABGAR KING OF ARMENIA

Converted to Christianity in A.D. 34. Baptised by the Apostle Thaddeus.

The wonderful cures and miracles of Christ were reported to him by the representatives he had sent to the Roman General Marinus in Jerusalem. These representatives had gone to refute the charges brought against him by King Herod, and to propitiate the Roman Power; they came back to tell what they had witnessed in Jerusalem, of the singular wisdom and wondrous works of a marvellous man named Jesus, who was of Nazareth, but whom his own followers persisted in calling the Son of God.

The story relates that Abgar was deeply impressed by what he heard, and expressed his own belief that man could not do such wondrous works as were related of this Jesus the Nazarene. Thereupon the King sent messengers to Jerusalem with a letter to Jesus. What a touch of human nature is here displayed; the king is suffering from a loathsome disease, the medical skill of his country and of neighbouring countries has been exhausted, all in vain; the royal heart is stricken as well as the royal body, for his disease is so loathsome, that although he is king, his subjects would rather shun than approach him; he hears of this wonderful man Jesus, his representatives have come back from Jerusalem to tell him that "he cleanseth the lepers." Hasten to him, said the king, take unto him my greetings, carry my messages and my letter and bring him unto me that I might honor him and if so be that he may heal me.

The messengers of Abgar were headed by Anany the Greek scribe of the king and they are supposed to be present in the procession of Christ's entry into Jerusalem. The twentieth and twenty-first verses of the Gospel of St. John are adduced by Armenian historians as corroborative testimony:

"And there were certain Greeks among them that came up to worship at the feast;

"The same came therefore to Philip, which was of Bethsaida of Galilee, and desired him, saying, Sir, we would see Jesus."

Anany and his companions are supposed to be the "certain Greeks" who came to Philip asking to see Jesus. And here I have to explain that the letters of the Armenian alphabet were invented by St. Mesrope in the beginning of the fifth century of the christian era; previous to the time of Mesrope there were no special Armenian letters, and as this invention was hailed as a signal national boon we have to conclude that there was no written Armenian language previous to the fifth century. One thing however must be certain, that this letter carried by the king's Greek scribe, the leader of the messengers, must originally have been written in Greek. This letter has already been translated from the Armenian into English; the translation reads thus:

"Abgar the son of Arsham, Prince of Armenia, sends to Thee, Saviour and Benefactor, Jesus, who didst perform miracles in Jerusalem, greeting.

"I have heard of Thee, and of the cures wrought by Thee without herbs or medicines; for it is reported that Thou restoreth the blind and maketh the lame walk, cleanseth the lepers, casteth out devils and unclean spirits, and healeth those that are tormented of diseases of long continuance, and that Thou also raiseth the dead:—hearing all this of Thee I was fully persuaded that Thou art the very God come down from heaven to do such miracles, or that Thou art the Son of God and so performeth them; wherefore I write to Thee to entreat Thee to take the trouble to come to me and cure my disease. Besides, I hear that the Jews murmur against Thee and want to torture Thee. I have a small and beautiful city—sufficient for us both."

The story goes on to relate that among the messengers was an artist by the name of John who had been commissioned by the king to bring back a portrait of Christ; the artist however failed in his efforts to portray the divine features, whereupon Christ gave him a veil which he had laid to his face and on which his features had become imprinted, to carry back to his master.

We are also told that the apostle Thomas was commanded by Christ to write a reply to Abgar. The reply has also been translated into English and the translation reads thus:

"Blessed is he who believes in Me without seeing Me, for it is written of Me that they that see Me shall not believe, and they that have not seen Me shall believe and be saved. As concerning the request that I should come to thee, it becomes Me to fulfil all things for which I was sent, and when I have fulfilled those then I shall ascend to Him that sent me; but after my Ascension I will send one of my disciples, who shall cure thee of thy disease and give life to thee and to all those that are with thee."

Two stories are given of the cure of Abgar. According to one version he was healed on receiving the veil, according to the other, the apostle Thaddeus on coming to Armenia laid his hands on the king and cured him.

This story of the veil has been treated by certain scholars as a legend, especially as the Roman church has also got a somewhat similar story. We are of course not in a position to vouch for its truth or incorrectness, but it seems to me if all the miracles of Christ as related in the gospels are to be credited, this one also can be regarded as one out of many. If according to the gospel story water was turned into wine at the marriage feast in Cana, what is there incredible about the imprint of the divine features on a veil; and if the gospels assure us of the healing of many lepers there can be nothing astonishing in the healing of the king of Armenia.

I was however much interested when I came across the following passage in the history of the "Spread of Islam":

"To the east they advanced to the banks and sources of the

Euphrates and Tigris; the long disputed barrier of Rome and Persia was forever confounded; the walls of Edessa and Amida, of Dara and Nisibis, which had resisted the arms and engines of Sapor or Nushirvan, were levelled in the dust; and the holy city of Abgarus might vainly produce the epistle or the image of Christ to an unbelieving conqueror."

"The long disputed barrier of Rome and Persia" which was "forever confounded" was of course Armenia; and "the holy city of Abgarus" the historian evidently had in his mind must have been Edessa, whither Abgar had removed his seat of government. To Armenians, however, Edessa has never been "the holy city," if they had a holy city, they would prefer to name Ani, the city of a thousand churches, or on account of its peculiar associations Etchmiatzin the ecclesiastical metropolis.

It was in Anno Domini 34 that the apostles Thaddeus and Bartholomew went to Armenia, where they were warmly welcomed and received with great reverence and respect by the King, who accepted the christian faith at once, himself and the royal household being baptised by the apostle Thaddeus.

Thaddeus and Bartholomew continued their preaching in Armenia, converting and baptising the people; churches were raised up, bishops consecrated, and the christian religion established in the country.

It might have been a matter of wonder to us why Saint Paul did not address an epistle to the Armenians as he addressed to other nations; but I think the 20th verse of the 15th chapter of his epistle to the Romans clearly explains the reason why there was not an epistle written to the Armenians also:

"Yea, so have I strived to preach the Gospel, not where Christ was named, lest I should build upon another man's foundation."

Clearly then no epistle was written to the Armenians because

Christ was already named among them, and Paul did not wish to build upon the foundation of Thaddeus and Bartholomew who had laid the foundation of Christianity in Armenia at a time when Paul himself was persecuting Christians. Thaddeus and Bartholomew left behind no epistles, and we have only Armenian history for the record of the work they did in Armenia.

Abgar died soon after his baptism and conversion, and was succeeded by his son Anany who tried to revive the old religion, which was something similar to the worship of the Greeks and Romans. The people of the country however had in large part accepted Christianity, and the revival of the old religion was consequently met with disfavour, but before their discontent had time to assume active tendencies Anany met his death by an accident; the people thereupon immediately invited Abgar's nephew Sanatrook to occupy the throne, taking a pledge from him that he would not interfere with their religion. The pledge was readily given by Sanatrook, but once secure on the throne he proved a cruel and merciless despot: the remaining sons of Abgar were killed, and his daughters and widow Helena banished, but the crowning act of the tyrant's wickedness and infamy was the martyrdom of the apostles Thaddeus and Bartholomew. Thus Christianity continued its struggles in Armenia, persecuted and declining, but still enduring.

About Anno Domini 260 the king reigning in Armenia by the name of Terdat, persecuted Christianity. He had regained his throne through the support of the Roman Army, and to celebrate his accession he offered thanksgiving and sacrifice in the temple of the goddess Anahid, which was no other than the goddess Diana of the Romans, but the fathers of the Armenian church in their christian zeal have reversed the name of the goddess, made a topsy-turvy of it, calling her Anahid, and so the name has remained in the Armenian language to this day.

This occasion of the king's worship and thanksgiving in the temple of Diana, marked the beginning of the persecution of Gregory, afterwards known as Gregory the Illuminator and the patron saint of Armenia. The childhood of Gregory had been shadowed by a parent's guilt: his father Anak having treacherously assassinated the then reigning king Khosrov the Great, the whole family was exterminated, only two sons escaping death, one of them, Gregory, was secretly removed by his nurse to Caesaria, and kept in concealment, until in the course of years the father's crime having been forgotten, all danger for the life of the son was supposed to have passed away.

SOORB GREGORE LOOSAVORITCH

(St. Gregory the Illuminator)

Patron Saint of Armenia. Revived Christianity in Armenia in A.D. 276.

Gregory's christian faith however now became the cause of his misfortunes; the king called upon Gregory to assist in the worship in the temple of Diana, but he firmly refused and boldly avowed his christianity, which so incensed the king that he ordered frightful tortures to be inflicted upon him, but as the tortures had no effect and Gregory remained firm to his faith, the king ordered him to be thrown into a dry well. The story goes on to relate that Gregory lived for fifteen years in this dry well, food and drink being conveyed to him secretly by a woman, herself a christian. On this spot is built the famous monastery of "Khorvirap" meaning "deep well."

A beautiful Roman maiden by the name of Rhipsimè fleeing from the addresses of the Emperor Diocletian sought refuge in Armenia; she was accompanied by a friend, a woman of maturer years of the name of Caiana, and some other christian maidens, all fleeing from persecution in Rome.

Rhipsimè's rare beauty had captivated the Roman emperor, and she had sought to escape from his passion by flight, but a crueller fate awaited her in Armenia, for king Terdat in his turn smitten by the exquisite beauty of her face offered to make her his queen, and her refusal to accept his throne and his love so exasperated the king that he ordered her beautiful head to be cut off. Thus Rhipsimè with Caiana and their young companions were cruelly martyred. Rhipsimè and Caiana were later beatified as saints in the Armenian church.

The king however did not escape the Nemesis of his diabolical crime, the memory of the beautiful Rhipsimè haunted him; remorse took the place of the ferocious anger that had doomed his hapless victim to her cruel death and the king lost his reason. The king having become incapacitated, Gregory was released from his underground prison by the king's sister Khosrovidookt, and as the malady of the king was mental, remorse for his own crime having overturned his reason, it became the peculiar office of Gregory to minister to the king, and by his spiritual ministrations to effect the restoration of the royal mind.

Terdat recovered his reason and as a broken-hearted penitent accepted the religion of Gregory and the beautiful Rhipsimè.

Gregory now freely preached Christianity in Armenia. It was a grand Revival; the temples of Anahid were turned into the churches of Christ, and the whole nation accepted Christianity, which became the established religion in the country.[18] The name of Gregory has been handed down to posterity as Soorb Gregore Loosavoritch (Saint Gregory the Illuminator). "Illuminator" is the generally accepted English translation of the Armenian term "Loosavoritch," but it is true nevertheless that neither the term "Illuminator" nor "Enlightener" suitably conveys the definition of its meaning; sometimes modes of expression are so difficult to translate from one language into another, and it can be said that

---

[18] The orthodox church of Armenia is the church founded by Gregory. Since the loss of their independence, persecution has scattered and dispersed the people, thousands fleeing from their native home sought refuge in other countries and in some cases they or their descendants have come under the influence of other churches; thus the Mukhitharian monks of the monastery of St. Lazar in Venice have been drawn into the Romish Church and their influence has been extended over a small minority of laymen; also the influence of the American Missionaries in Asiatic Turkey has drawn others into Protestantism, but the bulk of the nation has remained Gregorians. It is well to remark here however that the orthodox Church, although calling herself "The Holy Catholic and Apostolic Church" has devoted her energies mainly to upholding the essential principles of Christianity and has not concerned herself much about dogmas. As for the modern Armenians of the Gregorian Church their religious views are characterized by liberalism, they look to the central figure of Christianity and regard dogmas as immaterial: their jealousy of their church is only actuated by the passionate feeling of preserving nationalism. They regard their church as the ark in which nationalism may be preserved until the dawn of better days.

the term "Illuminator" is used for want of a better word in English. The Armenians call their religion "loois havat;" the word "loois" means "light" and "havat" means "faith" or "religion," but if I translated the two words as "enlightened faith" or "enlightened religion" the translation would not suitably convey the meaning of the original.

THE CATHEDRAL OF ETCHMIATZIN

(Only Begotten Descended)

Seat of the Supreme Patriarch. The foundation stone was laid by St. Gregory the Illuminator who built the Church in the third century of the Christian era.

The cathedral of Etchmiatzin is identified with Gregory; its name "Etchmiatzin" means in the Armenian language "the only begotten is descended," and the story attached to it is, that in a vision Christ appeared to Gregory descended in light; Gregory built his church on the spot where the vision had appeared to him, giving it the name of "Etchmiatzin" (only begotten descended). The cathedral also gives its name to the town Etchmiatzin, the ecclesiastical metropolis of Armenia.

Since the time of Gregory, Christianity has been the national religion of the Armenians, and they have clung to their christian faith through unremitting persecutions and martyrdoms such as no other christian people have been called upon to endure.

The cathedral of Etchmiatzin built by Gregory still stands to-day; it has constantly been repaired and rebuilt in some part or other, until perhaps little of the original building may be left, but it still claims to be the church built by the patron saint of Armenia. I shall here quote a passage from "Historical Sketch of the Armenian Church," written by an Armenian priest:

"Owing to political circumstances the Armenian Patriarchate had at times to be transferred to metropolises and to other principal towns of Armenia. In the year A.D. 452 it was removed to Dwin, in 993 to Ani, in 1114 to Rômklah, and in 1294 to Sis. The Kingdom of Cilicia becoming extinct, and, we having no more a kingdom and no longer a capital town, it was natural and proper to re-transfer the See to its own original place, as the entire nation unanimously desired it. Accordingly, in the year 1441, it was decided by an ecclesiastical meeting that the seat of the Catholicus should return to Holy Etchmiatzin, where to this day has been preserved the proper unbroken succession from our Apostles and from our holy Father, St. Gregory the Illuminator."

I read the other day in one of the foreign papers published in Japan, the following piece of news:

"An Armenian Church pronounced by experts to date from the

second century of the Christian era, has been discovered in a fair state of preservation in the neighbourhood of Bash-Aparnah."

Perhaps the excavations in Armenia which Professor Marr is now conducting might lead to throwing more light on Armenian history.

www.ingramcontent.com/pod-product-compliance
Lightning Source LLC
Chambersburg PA
CBHW011256040426
42453CB00015B/2424